CROSS-EXAMINATION

Cross-Examination

A PRACTICAL HANDBOOK

GEORGE COLMAN, Q.C.
A JUDGE OF THE SUPREME COURT OF SOUTH AFRICA

JUTA & COMPANY, LIMITED
CAPE TOWN   WYNBERG   JOHANNESBURG
1973

First Edition: 1970
Second Impression: 1973

ISBN 9781533096500

PRINTED IN THE REPUBLIC OF SOUTH AFRICA BY THE RUSTICA PRESS
(PTY.) LTD., WYNBERG, CAPE

PREFACE

In pursuit of the limited aims described in the first chapter of this book I have made free use of examples. Many of those are based, in some measure, upon actual cross-examinations. But, with one exception, they have been changed so fundamentally that what appears here is vastly different from what really happened. The witness in the exceptional example is no longer alive.

Thus any Mr., Mrs. or Miss Black, White, Brown, Green, or anyone else who fears (or hopes) that he or she has been quoted or depicted here is mistaken.

I would add an observation about the chapter headings: The subject does not lend itself to orderly classification, and nearly every chapter contains matter which does not, strictly speaking, fall within the scope of its heading. There is also a good deal of overlapping. In 'Preparation', for example, there is an example which could well have appeared in 'Material' or 'Timing'; and much that could have appeared under the heading 'Experts' will be found in other chapters.

The book cannot, therefore, be used as if it were a work of reference. Such benefits as it offers will be gained from a reading of the work as a whole.

The Meat in the Sausage Roll

(A NOTE TO THE 1973 REPRINT)

Among the readers who have spoken to me about this book, a surprisingly large number have told me that they did not trouble to read the first chapter.

That, in some cases, seems to have happened because it was thought that if I had said anything worth saying at the beginning of the book, I was bound to have repeated it further on. Others seem to have assumed that the book was analogous to the commercial sausage roll, into which one has to bite deeply if one wishes to get to the meat.

Both assumptions are wrong. One of the reasons for the brevity of the book is my belief (not shared by all lawyers) that, if a point has been clearly made, it gains nothing from reiteration. Another is that I have tried to avoid the sort of padding, not unfamiliar in expository works, whereby a morsel of nutriment can be made to take on the appearance, and command the price, of a heavy meal.

In the second part of Chapter I there is a brief, but important, discussion of the technique of multiple aims, which is one of the most valuable devices at the disposal of the cross-examiner. If there is anything in the book which is worth pondering, it is that.

G.C.
1973

CONTENTS

Preface · v
The Meat in the Sausage Roll · vii
I   Objects · 1
II   Ethics · 13
III   Preparation · 26
IV   Material · 46
V   Unarmed Combat · 67
VI   Risks · 87
VII Honest Witnesses · 102
VIII Experts · 121
IX   Timing · 153
X   Private Eye · 170

Chapter I
Objects

A. THE OBJECTS OF THIS BOOK

Cross-examination, skilfully employed, is perhaps the most useful of all the instruments used in the administration of justice. Difficult though it may be, at times, to ascertain the law and apply it correctly, it is very often even more difficult to establish the facts upon which a just decision must be based. In disputes and inquiries which depend upon the evidence of witnesses, there is frequently the danger that the testimony offered may be untruthful. And, even more often, it can be misleading because it is mistaken, or presented in an incomplete or inaccurate form.

The function of cross-examination is to eliminate or reduce the danger that, for such reasons as these, a false conclusion will be reached; and, often, there is no other way of achieving that result. It is, indeed, a matter for regret that it is in so narrow a field that this powerful technique for the elucidation of facts is available. If politicians were subject to cross-examination on what they said, their statements would be different and more helpful; and that is true also of journalists and advertisers. Possibly if the celebrated Dr. Kinsey's informants had been subject to cross-examination, his conclusions would have been different. But that is by the way. This book is concerned with the use of cross-examination in the places where it is permitted, namely in courts of law and in hearings before quasi-judicial tribunals.

GEORGE COLMAN, Q.C.

For the sake of simplicity, the fact-finding tribunal will be referred to throughout the book as 'the court'. That expression is intended to refer to the person or group of persons required to make findings of fact, whether he or it be a judge, a jury, a magistrate, an arbitrator, a commission, or any other person or body upon whom that function may have devolved. Similarly, the cross-examiner will be referred to as 'counsel' although it is not only barristers, but solicitors and others who are called upon to cross-examine witnesses.

If cross-examination were something capable of being taught (as, for example, mathematics is), and the present writer were qualified to teach it, neither apology nor explanation would be called for. But neither of these two premises is wholly true, and it is therefore appropriate to say something about the writer's limited aims, and the manner in which it is hoped that they may be achieved.

Although counsel may have to conduct important cross-examinations from the outset of his professional career, he usually faces that task without having had any substantial instruction or training in the technique. He learns it by experience, and if he becomes an able cross-examiner, his competence is the product of his experience, allied with his industry, his intelligence and his other personal gifts.

That, in large measure, is inevitable. Here, as in many other fields, there is no substitute for experience, and certainly no book or course of instruction can turn a person who lacks the necessary personal talents into a skilful cross-examiner. But there are things, normally learnt by experience, which are capable of formulation or illustration. And to those who have had little or no experience such formulation and illustration will surely be helpful.

It is such help that this work seeks to provide. To the seasoned practitioner, much that it contains will be familiar. But even he may find interest in and derive help from the analysis of techniques which he has, perhaps unconsciously, been employing. And he may find, in these pages, stimulating suggestions, or reminders of approaches which he has not been in the habit of using.

CROSS-EXAMINATION

Examples will be freely used to illustrate the points made. They will usually be fictitious ones, contrived for the purposes of this book; and even when they are not entirely fictitious, but are drawn from successful or unsuccessful cross-examination which the writer has heard, or has conducted, they will have been greatly modified. The main reason for this, and for the form which the fictitious examples take, is the need for simplicity. In practice, cross-examination is often a slower and more complicated process than these examples would suggest. But a more realistic presentation would not only lengthen the book unduly; it would tend to obscure the points which the examples are designed to illustrate. They should therefore be regarded, not as full and true reflections of what may happen between counsel and a witness, but as simplified and idealized indications of the process. They represent the bare bones which will, in an actual case, often be buried under a mass of superfluous flesh.

This, too, should be remembered about the examples: The witnesses who figure in them may seem unusually simple or compliant. Indeed, they are; the techniques which here yield such swift, clear and satisfactory results will not always do that before a court. The responses of the witness are likely, in practice, to be such as to call for much greater persistence from counsel; the ultimate achievement may be far less crisp; or the line of cross-examination may fail altogether to achieve any of its aims. A reader may be justified in suggesting that many of the examples reflect, not the real, hard world of the courts, but some sort of cross-examiner's paradise, where witnesses are tractable and dreams come true. But the examples are there to point to the aims, and to the possible results (not the inevitable ones), of the approaches which are being illustrated. It is no ground for despair, therefore, if the application of the techniques discussed in these chapters does not always, or often, yield the fruits which the examples seem to promise. That those techniques, or similar ones, sometimes succeed is the justification for this book.

There will be no examples of brilliant cross-examination, and no recipe for brilliance. Cross-examination of so high an order of

GEORGE COLMAN, Q.C.

skill as to deserve that epithet is rarer than many people think. And those who achieve it do so through their own industry, coupled with their own gifts. What this book seeks to offer is something less rare and less spectacular.

B. THE OBJECTS OF CROSS-EXAMINATION

It might seem unnecessary, in a work designed for the use of law students and counsel, to discuss the objects of cross-examination. Those who undertake to cross-examine, it might be thought, will at any rate know what they are about. But experience shows that often they do not. Nor, indeed, are the efforts of those who stand up and question witnesses without any clear appreciation of their aims always unsuccessful. Luck plays a part in cross-examination, as in so many other human activities. But it is the mark of the competent cross-examiner that he creates the situations in which openings and advantages, which may appear to be fortuitous, are likely to come his way. And when they do, he makes skilful use of them. If he is to do these things, it is well that he should be clear about his aims.

Really, there is one aim only. It is to assist in the administration of justice by revealing the truth to the court. It is no part of counsel's function to obscure or distort the truth, and a cross-examination which seeks to do that is an improper one. This might seem a naïve statement in the light of the well-known (and not entirely erroneous) dictum that the task of counsel is to make the worse case appear the better. But the dictum embodies a half-truth only. In a suit where both parties are represented by qualified and diligent counsel, before a conscientious and experienced tribunal (or one to which experienced guidance is available, as in the case of a jury), it is well that counsel on each side is striving to make his case appear the better one. Their honest efforts to do that are likely to reveal the truth; indeed, there is no other procedure which is so well adapted to produce that result.

In particular, when the result of a suit turns on the viva voce evidence of witnesses, cross-examination is invaluable. There are witnesses who testify, with the appearance of candour, to what they know to be false; there are witnesses who, because they are biased, or for other reasons, have deceived themselves into believing that what they say is true; there are witnesses who are honest, but mistaken; there are witnesses whose evidence in chief, although it is true and accurate, tends to mislead because material facts are omitted, or because undue emphasis has been laid upon some parts of their testimony and too little emphasis on others; there are witnesses whose evidence ought to be received with caution because of their temperaments, their habits, their history, or their interests. And there is no court, however wise and experienced, which can hope to avoid errors arising from the testimony of such witnesses, if there has been no competent cross-examination.

Unhappily, it cannot be said that cross-examination, even if thorough and skilful, will always reveal, unmistakably, the truth for which the court is seeking. But it cannot be doubted that, very often, it will. And the more competent the cross-examination is, the more likely it is that that result will be achieved. That, of course, is not to say that an able cross-examination will always destroy or weaken the evidence of the witness to whom it is directed. If the witness is speaking truthfully and accurately, so that, in the interests of justice, his evidence ought to be accepted, cross-examination is likely to reveal that fact. It is paradoxical that a cross-examination which has failed utterly from the point of view of cross-examining counsel (or, more properly, of his client) may have succeeded in its true purpose, from the court's point of view, in that it has helped to show clearly where the truth lies.

The broad statement that the purpose of cross-examination is to reveal the truth must, however, be broken down into subsidiary elements for the purposes of a work of this kind; and it is in relation to those subsidiary elements that the term 'objects of cross-examination' is used. The nature of those objects (or of the main ones) is indicated in the reference above to classes of witnesses whose testimony is likely to be accepted with reservations, if at all, after able cross-examination.

GEORGE COLMAN, Q.C.

The process is commonly thought of as one designed to expose the witness who is deliberately lying, and indeed it is that. But no less important is the achievement of counsel who demonstrates, by cross-examination, that a witness has been mistaken on one or more of the points in his evidence, or that he is biased, or otherwise unworthy of credence, or that material points have been omitted, or inadequately stressed, in the evidence in chief. And even when a cross-examination does not succeed in demonstrating matters of this kind, it is helpful if it reveals the probability (or sometimes even the possibility) that they exist. Courts work on probabilities of various degrees when certainty cannot be achieved; and although destruction of the evidence in chief constitutes success, a cross-examination may be equally valuable if it does no more than raise doubts about the reliability of the witness, or the accuracy of his evidence on a material point or points.

The task of counsel would appear to be much easier when the evidence is such that he can confine himself to one of these possible aims. But that is not wholly true. Certainly his problem is simpler when he knows that all he can hope to achieve with a witness is a simple, clear-cut result (for example, a concession that the witness was, or might have been, mistaken about a date which he mentioned in his evidence in chief). In the more common case, where counsel should approach the witness with multiple aims, a much higher order of concentration, awareness and alertness is called for.

An example of multiple aims is the case where counsel seeks, if he can, to show that the witness is a deliberate liar, but hopes, if he cannot show that, to elicit something else in his client's favour; it may emerge from the cross-examination that the witness is biased, that he is a careless observer, that he is a person who tends to make unjustified inferences, that he has a bad memory, or that he is subject to some other defect which makes it dangerous to accept what he says. These, and other circumstances adverse to the acceptance of the witness's testimony, may emerge from what he says about the material facts in his evidence; but they may be drawn from him in response to questions about subsidiary matters, or about matters which are not relevant to the case at all. Failing successes of these kinds, the cross-examination may none the less be fruitful if it elicits facts favourable to the cross-examiner's case which have not yet been placed before the court, or even if it shifts the emphasis which was originally placed on some parts of the evidence as opposed to others.

The task of counsel who has to bear all these alternatives in mind, and be ready to abandon one aim for another as the situation demands from time to time, is certainly not a simple one. Yet the multiplicity of his aims is part of his strength. If you aim a single bullet at your target, and it misses, you fail; your prospects of success are greater if you release a charge of shot; and a single pellet may be enough to bring your quarry down.

The figure of speech is, however, not an apposite one. Though some cross-examinations do somewhat resemble the discharge of a handful of pellets in the general direction of the witness, in the hope that something will draw blood, the able cross-examiner leaves less to chance than that. Conscious of all the possible forms which his success may take, he looks for openings, and tries to create them. He frames questions which, if they do not lead to success in one form, are likely to produce it in another. And he does not always let the witness see what aim or aims he is pursuing.

Indeed, multiplicity of aims gives the cross-examiner great advantages over the unscrupulous witness. When such a witness perceives a purpose in a line of questioning, he will often deliberately give answers designed to defeat the purpose. But unless he is astute enough to perceive also the various alternative objects which the cross-examiner has in mind, he is likely, in seeking to close one door, to open others. Few untruthful witnesses have enough intelligence, knowledge and experience to escape this difficulty when the case permits multiple-aim cross-examination, and it is ably conducted.

Counsel should never mislead a witness, and the court should stop him if he tries to do so. That does not mean, however, that he must disclose his purposes to the witness. It is legitimate, therefore,

GEORGE COLMAN, Q.C.

for counsel to frame his questions in such a way that, although the witness thinks he is seeking one type of answer, he is actually hoping for another. There will be examples, later in this book, which illustrate the manner in which this can be done.

It must be remembered that the honest witness has nothing to fear from that type of approach. He is there to state what he knows, and to voice his ignorance or his doubts when he has them. He need not concern himself with counsel's object in framing a question; he gives his answer, let it lead where it may.

The following is a very simple example of multiple purposes in cross-examination:

A woman is accused of shoplifting. The case against her is that she lurked by the scarf counter in a large departmental store, picked up a scarf, and was putting it into her handbag when a saleswoman, who had seen all this from the glove counter about ten yards away, shouted. The accused then pulled out the scarf and dropped it on the counter. The accused has told her legal advisers that she fingered the scarf, but did not intend or attempt to steal it, and that she made no attempt to put it in her handbag. She has added that it would have been absurd for her to do this, because she would have been seen by a number of people who were standing by the scarf counter, close to her; one of these, she thinks, was a policeman in uniform.

Counsel for the defence, when he rises to cross-examine the witness who was at the glove counter, knows that it is unlikely in the extreme that he will get her to retract the statement that the accused was putting the scarf into a bag. But he must try to shake her testimony, and he frames some of his questions in the hope of showing either that the witness could not have seen clearly what she claims to have seen, or that, even if she could have seen what the accused was doing, she was a poor observer, or a person likely to jump to conclusions. Failing that, he hopes, at any rate, to get from the witness some support for the important evidence which his client will give about the bystanders. He thinks that he is most likely to succeed on the last-mentioned point, but fears that if he

CROSS-EXAMINATION

approaches it directly the witness may go out of her way to destroy it, not necessarily because she is a liar, but because, like most witnesses, she will be reluctant to admit anything which will render her own testimony improbable. (Of the vanity of witnesses, more will be said later in this book.)

Thus, if counsel tackles the point directly, he may fail, in some such manner as this:

Will you agree that it would have been foolish for the accused to try to steal the scarf as you say she did?
I think it's always foolish to steal, but she did it.
But the circumstances made this sort of attempt particularly foolish, didn't they?
What circumstances?
Were there not a number of people close to the accused who were bound to see what she was doing?
There weren't many people about, and none of them was looking at the accused.
How can you be so sure of that?
I saw it. I have the picture in my mind now.
Was there not a policeman about?
Not near the accused. I'd have noticed him.

A more hopeful approach is this one:

Can you be mistaken about what the accused did with the scarf?
No.
You didn't watch her carefully, did you?
Well, I happened to be looking straight at her, and I saw exactly what happened.
But weren't you attending to your own customer?
I had none at that time.
Did you have a good view of the scarf counter?
Perfect.
And do you claim to be very observant?

GEORGE COLMAN, Q.C.

I'm pretty observant: I'm interested in people and I notice them and what they do.

Well, let us test your observation. Do you remember anything about the accused's shoes?

There was nothing special or relevant about the shoes. This question, and the next one, are designed to put the witness on her mettle about her powers of observation.

No. I didn't say I noticed every tiny detail.

Maybe you are not as observant as you think: Did you notice whether the clock on the wall near the entrance was going?

No. It was some distance from the glove counter.

Can I take it that you did notice what was near the glove counter, and was not a tiny detail?

Yes.

Did you notice a woman in a red coat about two yards from the accused?

Yes, I did.

Did you notice two men on the other side of the accused?

Yes.

Did these four people all form a little group near the end of the scarf counter?

Yes.

They all had their backs to you?

No. The man nearest the accused stood sideways and I could see through the gap.

You mean a small gap between his chest and the accused's left-hand side?

Yes.

And just before you shouted did you notice another person who came close to that group?

I think I did.

You think you did? Let me help you. Did you, a pretty good observer, with a clear view, see anyone in uniform near the accused?

Well...yes. ...There was someone in uniform.

A policeman?

I'm not sure he was a policeman.

CROSS-EXAMINATION

But you're not sure he wasn't?
I don't think he was a policeman.
*I'm asking you what you're sure about. You said you were not sure he was
a policeman. And if you're not sure, he may have been?*
Well, I suppose he may have been.

This is a considerable measure of success from the cross-examiner's point of view. How much further he can take it, and in what manner, will depend upon his assessment of the witness. He will, by now, have been able to form some view of her, and on the basis of that view he may be able fruitfully to pursue one or more of his multiple aims.

He might ask what the bystanders, and in particular the man in uniform, did when the witness shouted. The answers to questions on this subject may show that the accused was, indeed, so clearly under the eyes of a policeman and others that it is unlikely that she would have committed the crime. Or they may show that the witness was not a reliable observer. She may testify to conduct on the part of others which is so improbable as to throw doubt upon her own testimony. She may, in trying to avoid improbabilities in her testimony, make conflicting statements, or reveal bias on her part. Another possibility, of course, is that the witness will show herself to be fair-minded and reasonable, and will impress the court with her reliability; but, as has been pointed out, not every cross-examination can, or should, succeed; and if the witness's evidence is ultimately accepted, the cross-examination has not brought that about; she would, presumably, have been believed if there had been no cross-examination at all.

Because of the important part that the multiple aim often plays in successful cross-examination, it will be exemplified further in later chapters. To conclude this one a simple example, familiar to all pracitioners, will suffice.

When a witness has testified to an important, dramatic or interesting event in which others, who may also give evidence, took part, or which they saw or heard, it is often useful to question him about subsequent discussions with those others.

GEORGE COLMAN, Q.C.

And when you got home, did you and your brother talk about the accident?

A negative reply might cast doubt upon the candour of the witness, if the event was one which they would almost certainly have discussed. Moreover, the brother, if called, may give a different answer. If the witness answers affirmatively, the cross-examination may continue:

> *Was his recollection the same as yours?*
> Yes.
> *On every point?*
> Yes.
> *Had he noticed anything which you hadn't noticed?*
> Nothing.
> *Did you agree on every single detail which you have mentioned in your evidence?*
> Yes.

Three possibilities flow from this: The brother may not be called, and that may found a valid criticism of the litigant who could have been expected to call him. Or he may be called, and his testimony may differ from that of this witness, and a criticism may be based on that. If he is called, and his evidence does coincide completely with that of this witness, it may be argued that it is unlikely that two observers of a sudden and unforeseen event will notice and remember exactly the same things, and that it is more probable that some, at least, of the testimony is based not on direct observation, but upon what passed in conversation between the two brothers, so that what appears to be strong confirmation is nothing of the kind.

If the witness, in response to the questions, says that his brother's recollection did not coincide fully with his own, the matter can be probed further, and the impressiveness of one or both of the observers may well be weakened in consequence of what emerges.

Chapter II
Ethics

Legal procedure gives a cross-examiner great privileges. Within wide limits, he may ask what he pleases, and the witness is compelled to answer him. He is often in a position, without fear of any adverse consequences to himself, to hurt or humiliate a witness, to pry into his private concerns, or to injure his reputation. Sometimes it is the cross-examiner's duty to do these things. But his privileges carry with them corresponding moral obligations. The law places certain limitations upon what a cross-examiner may do; and the court, in the exercise of its discretion, can impose further restrictions. But even in relation to matters well within those bounds, it is the duty of counsel to exercise his rights, as a cross-examiner, with fairness, moderation, taste and discretion. This applies both to the manner and to the matter of a cross-examination.

The manner in which a witness is addressed will often have an effect upon the answers which he gives. And it is right for counsel to vary his manner as circumstances require. His duty to his client may make it necessary for him, at times, to use a tone of voice or a form of words which courtesy would restrain him from using on a social occasion. But he should carry his courtesy into the courtroom with him; and he should deviate from it only when, and to the extent that, a deviation is necessary for the proper conduct of his case.

To bully a witness is never justified. And it is seldom, if ever, proper to shout at one. These are bad tactics, as well as bad manners. The answer which has been hammered out of a cowed witness by a hectoring cross-examiner will not have the weight which the same answer would have had if it had been extracted by gentlemanly means.

That is not to say that firmness is never called for. Witnesses are often wilfully or inadvertently evasive or irrelevant. And it is a weak cross-examiner who does not insist, in most instances, upon an answer to a question which he has asked, if the witness is able to answer it. The exceptional case is the one where the witness, by avoiding the question, has given counsel what he wants. More effective sometimes than

'I insist that you answer my question'.

is

'I have put my question three times, and each time you have talked about something else. Would you prefer me to drop the question?'

This is likely to produce either an answer to the question which the witness has been evading, or an admission that the witness does not wish to answer it, which may be sufficient for counsel's purposes.

But even when an answer is required, it is seldom necessary to shout at the witness, or to rebuke him in strong terms. This sort of thing, in crescendo, may appeal to the gallery:

How dare you trifle with me, Mr. Black? I'll have that answer out of you or you'll find yourself in jail. Come on, answer me, Sir, answer me!

But the desired result is more properly, and often more effectively, obtained by a quieter method:

Did you see the traffic light?
I always look carefully for traffic lights, wherever I go.
Did you see the traffic light?
I was looking ahead of me. I mean there was nothing to distract me. Of course I had to concentrate on the cyclist ahead, and see if there was any oncoming traffic.

CROSS-EXAMINATION

(In a firmer tone, but not a shout)

Did you see the traffic light?

With a witness who is believed to be honest, even though mistaken, a friendly, conversational tone is often the best one. A courteous series of reasonable suggestions, put, perhaps, with a smile here and there, may evoke more candid answers than the ones which would be given in response to a stern cross-examination. But, unhappily, it is not every witness who will respond in that way. Some, though fundamentally truthful, will be careless of the accuracy of their answers unless the cross-examiner's tone reminds them of the solemnity of the occasion. And with many untruthful witnesses, little can be achieved unless they are kept on a tight rein.

In the chapter on Experts the reader will find an example of the cross-examination of a professor of English literature, in which the cross-examiner achieves a substantial measure of success by means of questions which are, almost without exception, good-humoured in their phrasing, and which could effectively be put in a good-humoured tone of voice. But other tones of voice are needed in other circumstances. The primary purpose of a question is to elicit information from the witness which will be helpful to counsel's case. But it is often necessary or desirable to phrase and enunciate a question so as to convey something to the witness, such as surprise, disapproval, disgust or disbelief, which is likely to affect his immediate and subsequent answers. Thus, when a witness has said—

I had no doubt about it.
No doubt at all? (In tones of surprise),

may well lead the witness to say—

Well, I was fairly sure, anyway.

GEORGE COLMAN, Q.C.

When a witness has given an untruthful account of an assault which he claims to have seen, as an innocent passer-by, it may be legitimate to ask, in somewhat horrified tones:

So you left this poor girl bleeding on the pavement while you walked on to your game of cards?

The tone of voice may serve this purpose: It may make the witness feel so uncomfortable that he will invent some addition to his already untruthful story. And the more he invents the more likely it is that counsel will be able to demonstrate his untruthfulness.

In contrast to this it should be stressed that it is improper to sneer at a witness who has not said or done anything to invite contempt. To mock the pronunciation or the faulty grammar of a witness is inexcusable. Indeed, counsel's tone of voice and choice of language should never be designed to make a witness feel uncomfortable unless the witness has done or said something which deserves it. When counsel, addressing the keeper of a small suburban shop, refers to the shop as 'your emporium' that is usually vulgarity, not advocacy.

That does not mean, however, that the use of irony has no place in cross-examination. As will be pointed out in a later chapter, irony (related not to the witness personally, but to the content of his evidence) is sometimes appropriate and useful.

Counsel should not interrupt the witness's answer needlessly, even if it seems as if he is being irrelevant; and he should certainly not interrupt because he realizes or fears that the answer, if completed, will be adverse to him. If it is plain that the witness has misunderstood the question, or is for some other reason giving a lengthy answer which is off the point, an interruption may be necessary. But it can be made politely, in some such words as these:

One moment, please. You are talking about what happened before Xmas. I wanted to know what happened this year.

CROSS-EXAMINATION

or

> *Please, Mr. Green. You were not asked to give the names of all your employees. Let me repeat the question: How many employees did you have?*

It should be remembered, however, that witnesses are seldom adept in logical exposition. What seems irrelevant may be leading up to the answer called for. It should be remembered, also, that the uncalled-for statement by a witness is the very thing which, followed up, may lead to his destruction. Sometimes the best course is to let him talk.

Nor, in general, should a witness be hurried. Some people think slowly or speak hesitantly. And in any event, a man who has sworn to speak the truth should be allowed to think before he speaks, at any rate if the matter is one about which there is room for reflection. But there are instances in which counsel is justified in requiring a prompt reply. They include the occasion upon which a witness, putting forward what counsel believes to be a fabricated story, makes a slip which should be followed up quickly:

Black, White and Brown are charged with joint participation in a robbery, and Brown (a man of low intelligence) is testifying in his own defence. He says that he took no part in the crime, and that although he knew Black and White, he had not been in their company on the day of the robbery, or for several weeks before it. Prosecuting counsel cross-examines him at some length about the nature of his association with White, and comes to this point:

> *Did you and he go out together?*
> Sometimes.
> *Where did you go?*
> He took me to a couple of parties.
> *Where else?*
> Once he took me to the races.
> *Where else?*
> (After a pause). He took me into trouble.

This is the slip. Counsel exploits it quickly.

> *Trouble? What trouble?* (Short pause)—*Come on, you must know; what trouble? This trouble?*
> Yes.
> (Quickly and insistently)—*He took you to the scene of this crime?*
> (Faintly)—Yes.
> (Quickly)—*You were there. You had the revolver. Black had the car. Isn't that so?* (Short pause)—*Isn't that so?*
> (Sadly)—Yes.

In this example counsel's success was the result, in part, of Brown's dull-wittedness, and in part of counsel's strong personality, a gift of nature. But it was the result, in large measure, of counsel's quick appreciation of the weakness, and his firm insistence on prompt answers to his simple questions. In the circumstances, it was entirely fair and proper for him to press his questions rapidly and insistently, so as to cut down the time for invention.

The subject-matter of cross-examination is not confined to what is in issue between the parties. Counsel may cross-examine a witness as to character and (subject to the court's discretion to prevent abuse) on almost anything else for the purpose of testing credibility. But here, too, there are important ethical limitations. There should be no attack upon the character of a witness, or upon any aspect of his morality, unless his character or credibility are really in issue. Nor should counsel use his privilege to pry into the private affairs of a witness unless he has good reason to believe that they are relevant to an issue in the case, or that the answers may throw light upon the character or credibility of the witness where credibility is material. It is unjustifiable, in the absence of any such purpose, to ask a man whether he has been convicted of a crime, or whether he is married to the woman who shares his flat.

Suggestions of untruthfulness or of improper conduct should not be made to a witness unless counsel has good grounds for thinking that they are well founded. When he has no more than suspicions, or ill-verified information, he should feel his way carefully with the witness. If it turns out that his suspicions were justified, the revelation may well be more effective than it would have been in response to a direct question, as the following example may illustrate:

Counsel, who has to cross-examine a witness called J. White, believes that he has recently come out of jail, having spent six months there for perjury. If that is so, it should be elicited, as the evidence of the witness is to be disputed by counsel's client. There is no certainty, however, that it is not another man called J. White who was in jail for perjury, and the cross-examination is opened with proper caution:

Mr. White, where were you living during January of this year?
I've had my house at Baker Street ever since the war.
But did you eat and sleep there during January of this year?
No.
Why not?
I was away from home.
Where were you?

The witness asks the court whether he must answer the question. The court, having been assured by counsel that he has a valid reason for putting the question, tells the witness to answer it.

I was in an institution. Counsel is now reasonably sure of his ground. But he refrains from putting his information directly because the witness is destroying his own credibility. He asks:

What sort of institution?
It was a prison.
For how long were you there?
I'm not sure: several weeks.
Why were you there?
I was wrongly convicted. I made some mistakes.
In an affidavit?

Yes, I think that's what you call it.

So you are the J. White who was convicted in November of last year of perjury and sentenced to six months' imprisonment?

Yes.

Subject to the limitations which have been and will be indicated, counsel may put to the witness any theory which occurs to him about a matter upon which the witness is or may be able to testify. And he is under a duty to put to him what counsel's own witnesses will say if it conflicts with the testimony of the witness under cross-examination. That should be done in sufficient detail to enable the witness to correct his mistakes, if he has made any, or to explain the apparent conflict, if there is an explanation. But counsel must be careful, in so doing, not to deceive or mislead the witness. It is improper to put or suggest to a witness that there is evidence to contradict him if that evidence does not exist, or is not available to counsel. Thus, to a witness who has said—

I am almost certain that I signalled my intention to turn. it is improper to say—

There are three witnesses who will swear that you did not. What do you say now?

unless there are in fact three witnesses ready to swear positively to that fact. The question would not be justified by the fact that the witnesses were ready to say, for example, that they do not remember seeing a signal, or that it is their impression that none was given.

This applies equally to what may be called real evidence. The question:

What would you say if I told you that your fingerprints were found on the letter?

is justified only if counsel is able to prove that the prints on the letter are those of the witness. If counsel suspects, on reasonable

CROSS-EXAMINATION

ground, that they are, and is awaiting expert evidence to support or negative his suspicion, he is entitled to go no further than this:

> *There are fingerprints on the letter. I am having them examined by an expert, who may find that they are yours. Do you still say that you never handled the letter?*

In a published work there is an account of a successful cross-examination of a witness who had sworn that he saw something happen by moonlight. Having elicited from the witness that the moon was bright, counsel produced a printed almanac and directed the attention of the witness to an indication therein that there was no moon on the night in question. The witness thereupon admitted that the whole of his evidence was a fabrication. In fact the almanac was a false one, which counsel had had printed for the specific purpose of trapping the witness into an admission that he had lied. He no doubt thought that as the witness was, in fact, a perjurer, the end justified the means adopted by him. In the opinion of the present writer, counsel was guilty of gross misconduct.

To put to a witness, even accurately, the extrajudicial statement of a person who has not been and will not be a witness in the case, is improper unless the extrajudicial statement is, on some ground, receivable in evidence, and is to be proved. The temptation to do that is sometimes strong, and counsel may feel frustrated when he would like to put a question like this one to a witness who claims to have been absent from a particular gathering:

> *But the Bishop has said that he saw you there. I'm not calling him to say so, because he is abroad. But he is quite positive that you were there. Do you suggest that he is lying?*

The witness is free to answer:

> Unless he comes here and says it, I shan't accept that he has ever made such a statement.

But that does not justify the question. By asking it counsel has conveyed to the court information which might influence it, and which it ought not to receive.

It is similarly improper for counsel to put a question, which he knows that his opponent will rightly object to, so that it will never be answered; that is sometimes done, not because an answer is hoped for, but because the mere utterance of the question will have some effect upon the mind of the court, or the witness. That effect will not be obliterated by the successful raising of an objection after the question has been asked, and the gain to counsel's client may be substantial. But it is unscrupulous to seek an advantage by such means.

Another type of misconduct which cross-examining counsel must scrupulously avoid is the misrepresentation to a witness of what he himself has said. A witness may not remember clearly what he has said in earlier stages of a long cross-examination; still less may he remember what he said when testifying on some previous occasion. Thus if, at one stage, a witness has said:

His conduct certainly didn't please me.

it is improper to put to him at a later stage—

> *But why, then, did you tell the court yesterday that you were angry with him?*

It is, in subtler instances than the one cited as an example, easy for counsel to fall into such an error inadvertently. There is a tendency, involuntarily, to paraphrase a vague answer favourably to oneself, or to remember a statement without its troublesome qualification. But, for that very reason, care is necessary to ensure that the previous answer is not being misquoted or distorted.

Another type of distortion which must be avoided arises in this way: A long question is asked, and the witness, when he comes to give his answer, has forgotten all except the last part of it, or is

CROSS-EXAMINATION

unable to frame an answer which responds to the question as a whole. A cross-examiner should never seek to take advantage of such an error when he sees or suspects that it has been made. It is, in fact, his duty to frame his question with sufficient clarity and conciseness to ensure that the witness understands what he is answering, and is able to formulate the answer which he wishes to give.

A less serious misuse of cross-examination, but one which should be avoided, is the introduction, under the guise of questions, of what is in truth argument. In some degree, that can hardly be avoided; and, indeed, it is sometimes perfectly proper to give a witness the opportunity of meeting a submission which counsel has it in mind to make about his evidence. Thus:

> *Unless you tell me from whom you received that piece of news, I shall probably submit to the court, in due course, that you didn't receive it at all. Now, from whom was it?*

But it is quite a different thing to address a witness thus:

> *I put it to you that you are the most unmitigated blackguard who ever entered this courtroom.*

That is not a question. Counsel expects no answer from the witness which can be of the slightest help to anyone. Although such assertions are often made to witnesses, one wonders whether they have any purpose unconnected with the presence of a newspaper reporter in the courtroom, or counsel's delight in the sound of his own voice.

Enough has been said to illustrate the principle that cross-examination must be fair, and that the witness must not be misled. But that is not to say that counsel is always under an obligation to reveal his purposes to the witness. On the contrary, one of the advantages which a cross-examiner legitimately enjoys is that the witness often fails to discern the plan underlying the cross-examination, or to understand where his answers are leading him.

GEORGE COLMAN, Q.C.

A question so framed that the witness does not know which answer counsel would prefer is often the one most likely to reveal the truth. Thus, provided that his question is a proper one, clearly and fairly formulated, counsel is under no obligation to respond to the not unfamiliar plea from the witness-box:

I don't see what that is leading up to.

He is entitled to say:

Don't concern yourself with that. You understand the question. Please answer it.

An ethical question which may be raised is whether it is proper for counsel so to frame his questions as to encourage an untruthful witness to add to or magnify his lies. There are suggestions, in this book, that in certain circumstances that should be done. There are illustrations, also, of the manner in which counsel may make use of the vanity of a witness, or his imaginativeness or suggestibility, to elicit answers on the basis of which he will later argue that the evidence in chief of that witness should not be accepted. How, it may be asked, are these things reconcilable with the proposition that the purpose of cross-examination is to establish the truth?

The reconciliation lies here: It is not claimed that the aim and duty of the cross-examiner is to obtain a truthful answer from every witness to every question asked. With some witnesses that is, indeed, what counsel tries to achieve. And it would be a happier world in which there were some method of achieving it with all witnesses. But that is not this world. There are witnesses who consciously lie, and cannot be made to tell the truth. There are witnesses who give unreliable answers because of their vanity, prejudice, irresponsibility, bias, or inability to distinguish between observation and inference, or between reality and imagination.

The proper administration of justice requires that the court which will have to weigh up the evidence of such a witness should be aware of his tendencies or weaknesses. That is the truth which counsel is seeking to make plain when he purposely elicits from such a witness an answer which is manifestly untruthful, exaggerated, or inaccurate. If regard is had to that purpose, and to the circumstances in which it is pursued, the suggestion of impropriety is refuted.

One of the circumstances postulated is that the court is alert and intelligent. If it is, it will understand fully what is happening before it, and it will not necessarily discard the whole of the testimony which a witness has given merely because some of his answers were clearly false or inaccurate. Nor will it necessarily accept as true an answer extracted under cross-examination from a witness whom it judges to be unreliable. Courts, of course, vary in alertness and intelligence; and that is particularly so when the term 'court' is given the wide denotation which has been assigned to it in the first chapter of this book. But even before such a tribunal as a jury of average men and women, justice is best likely to be served if there is able argument by counsel following upon able cross-examination of the witnesses.

Chapter III
Preparation

From an analysis of successful cross-examinations it will appear clearly that in many instances counsel's success was attributable to careful preparation. An example is the case where an expert has been driven into an untenable position by the skilful use of a battery of authorities, supplemented, it may be, by quotations from the previous statements or writings of the witness. It will not always be enough, in such a case, that counsel be in possession of a number of extracts from technical writings which, on the face of them, seem to conflict with the testimony under attack. If evasions are to be dealt with effectively, counsel must have an understanding of the subject-matter; sometimes, indeed, he will be unable, without such an understanding, even to see clearly where and how the available technical material conflicts with what the witness is saying.

At the other end of the spectrum we find successful cross-examinations which, on the face of them, do not appear to have depended on preparation at all. A witness has been called whose testimony came as a surprise to counsel; there may have been no reason to expect even that there was such a witness. Yet, as the consequence of able questioning, the evidence given by the witness in chief has been destroyed or weakened.

In the production of such dramatic results, luck often plays a part. The successful cross-examiner will frequently admit that he does not know how he came to ask the question or series of questions which, in retrospect, can be seen to have brought about his success.

CROSS-EXAMINATION

Or it may be that it was the personality of counsel which, in some manner which is incapable of analysis, caused the witness to make admissions or display weaknesses which would never have emerged under questioning by equally able counsel with a different voice or appearance, or with different personal qualities of some kind. It is one of the weaknesses of a book like this one that such elements in successful cross-examination cannot be classified or described.

But preparation, in a broad sense, plays a greater part in the cross-examination, even of an unexpected witness, than many would think. If one gives the term its widest ambit, it can fairly be said that the whole of counsel's education and experience has been a part of his preparation for any cross-examination which he undertakes. His knowledge of law, which tells him what he wants from the witness, and his knowledge of human affairs and human nature, which tell him how to get it, are, in the ultimate analysis, the primary tools of his trade. To put the matter somewhat less broadly, an appreciation of the techniques described and the suggestions made elsewhere in this book (and of other, subtler techniques which counsel's intelligence and experience will teach him) is part of his preparation. It is perhaps illogical that this chapter appears so early in the work, because the preparation which it enjoins is preparation to use, as far as it may be applicable to the case which is being prepared, the advice offered in other chapters; and when that injunction has been tendered, there is not a great deal more to be said.

But there is room for some residual guidance, and that will be attempted here. To begin with, a distinction is drawn between what may be called general preparation and specific preparation. When it is known or expected that a particular witness will be called, and what he will say, or is likely to say, counsel will be wise to prepare, as thoroughly as he can, to deal with that witness; that is what is meant by specific preparation. But in order to deal with unexpected witnesses, and with the unforeseeable details in the evidence of expected witnesses, the preparation will be of a type which can be called general.

GEORGE COLMAN, Q.C.

The first essential is that counsel be fully familiar with the issues in the suit and with the law governing their resolution, so that he will have a clear appreciation of what he wants, or can hope helpfully to obtain, from the witnesses. That, like much else in this chapter, may appear to be obvious; but it is considered to be worth mentioning because some inexperienced counsel will undertake cross-examination with no more than a general understanding of the issues, and of the relevant law; a detailed study of these things, they think, can be deferred until after all the evidence has been heard. But if that is done, valuable opportunities may be missed. It must be remembered that a large part of the cross-examiner's function is to deal with, and, if possible, exploit the unexpected. Thus the proviso to a statutory provision or a refinement in the law which seems to be irrelevant at the stage of general preparation may become important when a witness gives an unexpected answer. But if counsel is unaware of the proviso or the refinement, he may not see his opportunity when it arises; and having failed to see it, he will not ask the questions which are necessary in order to make use of the opening which presents itself.

A crude illustration or two may be a helpful pointers to the less obvious applications of the thesis which has been put forward: In some jurisdictions agreements falling within certain categories are invalid if concluded on Sunday. Counsel is preparing to cross-examine the witnesses who will be called against his client in a dispute about the existence of such an agreement. Neither party is contending that the agreement was made on a Sunday: what is in dispute is whether the agreement was made at all. Yet, in the cross-examination of an unexpected witness, who claims to have been a bystander when the bargain was struck, questions designed to test the likelihood that the witness was there at all may throw up something like this:

What were you doing at the plaintiff's house when the defendant arrived?
I was just paying a social call.

CROSS-EXAMINATION

If counsel is unaware of the legal provision relating to agreements made on Sundays, he may see no point in taking the following line:

At about what time of day did the defendant arrive?
At about four o'clock in the afternoon.
What is your occupation?
I am a bank clerk.
Banks close at five, don't they?
Yes, but this was a Saturday or a Sunday afternoon.
And if I tell you that the plaintiff played golf every Saturday afternoon during that month?
Then it was a Sunday.

This could have one of two results. The plaintiff will say that the agreement was not made on a Sunday, in which case serious doubt is thrown on the truthfulness of his witness. Or, if the witness is likely to be accepted as truthful, counsel may be able, by amendment, to introduce the alternative defence that if there was an agreement, it is an unenforceable one because it was concluded on a Sunday.

Similarly, in a case where a witness to a dying declaration has to be cross-examined, counsel may miss an opportunity of showing that the evidence is inadmissible unless he is aware of the legal requirements that the declarant must have a 'settled, hopeless expectation of death, not qualified by any prospect of recovery, however slight' (*Phipson on Evidence*, 8th ed., p. 313). Alive to the requirement, he may question the witness thus:

It must have been distressing for you to hear him say 'I've had it; I'm bleeding to death'?
Of course.
Did you say nothing to cheer him up?
I tried: I said I was sure the ambulance would come soon, and they'd stop the bleeding at once.
Didn't that help?
Not really. He thought they might be too late.

What were his words?

He said 'If they're not here in ten minutes they'll be too late'.

You were not so cruel as to tell him that you knew they couldn't get there in ten minutes, were you?

No, of course not.

And was it immediately after that that he said that the accused had stabbed him?

The reason why it is important that counsel should have a detailed knowledge of all the issues in the case, even if the witness has been called to testify on one of them only, will be clear from the references, elsewhere in this book, to the multiple purposes of cross-examination.

As a further part of his general preparation, counsel should make himself familiar with all the material relevant to the case. The pleadings, the correspondence, and all the other documentary material should be closely studied. Counsel should make himself fully acquainted with the details, as well as the essential features, of the evidence which his own witnesses will or can give. Material objects which have a bearing upon the case should be examined carefully. And a close inspection of a place which will be referred to in evidence, is often well worth while.

The reason for the stress which is laid upon detailed study of the material is this: The features of the case which are directly material will probably be as familiar to the witness as they are to counsel. If he is lying, or if there is a flaw in his testimony, that is unlikely to reveal itself in answers related to those broad issues alone; a favourable result is far more likely to be achieved by close questioning on matters of detail. Fortunately for the administration of justice, even the most astute of perjurers are seldom able to fabricate in a manner consistent with all the surrounding details of the central incidents to which they depose. The evidence in chief of such a witness may be so carefully contrived that it seems to fit all the known facts. But usually it is possible, in cross-examination, to ask him questions which he has not expected. In order to deal with these, he may have

CROSS-EXAMINATION

to improvise. And in so doing, he is not unlikely to say something which counsel will be able to reveal as untruthful or improbable if he has a sufficient command of the surrounding detail.

When a witness has deposed, untruthfully, to an adultery which he claims to have seen through a keyhole, there is little purpose in asking:

> *Was your field of vision through the keyhole wide enough to enable you to see all that you have spoken of?*

Questions about how much of the room the witness could see, and all that he saw in it, may produce helpful results, even if counsel has no more than a vague idea of the scene. But if he has studied it carefully, he can frame his questions more purposefully. Thus:

> *When she took off her dress, where did she put it?*
> On a chair.
> *Was that the green chair by the looking glass?*
> No, the other chair. A brown one in the alcove.
> *Did she just drop it on the chair, or did she fold it?*
> She folded it.
> *Please demonstrate the way in which she did that.*

(The witness gives a convincing demonstration of a dress being laid across a chair and then folded up.)

> *Was there anything else on the chair?*
> No.
> *Did she put her stockings on that chair too?*
> No, she just dropped them on the rug.
> *Did they both fall on the rug?*
> Yes.
> *You saw them lying there?*
> Yes.
> *What was the colour of the rug?*

I don't remember. It was a dark colour. The stockings showed up against it.

And all this you saw by the light of the lamp on the bedside table?

I have already said so.

My witnesses will say, and we shall show the court, if necessary, that when the main light is off the alcove is in darkness. What do you say to that?

The alcove was in darkness, but the lady stood just outside it, and I could see by her movements how she was folding her dress.

But you couldn't see the chair. You have already told me that you have never been in the room, and that you have received no information from anyone else.

(Counsel had opened the cross-examination by extracting answers to that effect.)

How do you know it was a chair?

I inferred it. What else would people keep in such an alcove? And I could see that she was working at about chair height.

And you inferred also that it was a brown chair?

(The witness does not answer, and counsel may be content to press on to his next question.)

I shall prove that the rug on which you say you saw the stockings was below the level of vision of a person looking through the keyhole. You invented that piece of evidence, didn't you?

That was a careless witness. But perjurers often are careless. And so are honest witnesses who have been led astray by their faulty observations or faulty memories.

Among the many types of detail which can be used to test the reliability of evidence, dates and the sequence of events may be important. If the material events cover a lengthy period it may be rewarding if counsel prepares a chronological table of events and keeps it at hand while he is cross-examining. As witnesses cannot always remember dates accurately, and may be careless of them when fabricating, this sort of thing can happen:

Until you noticed the defect you had no reason for repudiating your purchase of the car?

No.

Did you notice the defect before or after your holiday at Seaville?

During my holiday.

How long were you away on holiday?

Three weeks.

So when you wrote your letter on 18th March saying that the car was not giving satisfaction, you had already had your holiday?

Yes.

Look at this paid cheque of yours. Was it issued at Seaville?

It must have been. It's stamped by a bank at Seaville.

And it's dated 29th April. Do you still say you noticed the defect during your holiday?

I must have been mistaken....Yes, I remember now, it was on another trip I took.

What trip?

A trip to Brownville.

When did you go there?

I'm not sure. Before my holiday.

Let me help you. Here is an advertisement in which Brownville Motors offer new model cars at a reduced price. You saw that, didn't you?

I can't remember ever having seen it.

Did you buy one of those cars from Brownville Motors?

Yes.

When I was there.

According to your ledger you paid the deposit for that car on 20th March; is that right?

Yes.

Now concentrate on these dates. The advertisement appeared on 17th March. The following day you wrote saying that your car was not giving satisfaction, but not repudiating the purchase. You then went to Brownville, and on 20th March you paid a deposit on another car. You got delivery after your holiday, and you then repudiated your purchase from the plaintiff. Was it because the car was giving trouble, or was it because you had acquired a better car more cheaply?

An appreciation of relevance is of immense assistance in preparing cross-examination, for reasons which are obvious. But there is this anomaly: it is unwise to withhold attention from all that appears, on the face of it, to be irrelevant. One of the reasons is that it cannot be predicted, at the time of preparation, what may become relevant when some unexpected witness is called, or when an expected witness gives an unpredictable answer. It is, of course, not very helpful to counsel to be reminded of this. There are limits to his time and energy, and he cannot be expected to qualify himself on every fact remotely connected with the issues in the suit with which he is concerned. Perhaps the most that can be asked of him, in relation to the material in his papers which seems entirely irrelevant, is this: that he should make himself familar with the broad nature of what it is, and where it is to be found, so that he can turn to it easily and quickly if, during the suit, it assumes a possible relevance.

Another reason for scrutinizing closely what appears, on the face of it, to be immaterial to the inquiry, is that close concentration may reveal a hitherto unsuspected relevance. That is what underlay the advice given long ago by a distinguished English judge to young counsel. 'Claw the facts', he said; and to one member, at least, of his audience, that proved a valuable injunction.

Thus, when preparing a chronological table of events as an aid to cross-examination, counsel should not confine himself to events which bear directly upon the issues. He should include events which he may find it useful to refer to in lines of cross-examination related only to the credibility of witnesses. But he should go further, even, than that. Within the limits of what is practical he should include, against their proper dates, events which seem, on the face of them,

CROSS-EXAMINATION

to be mere pieces of indisputable history. It can well happen that while doing this, or when studying his table after he has completed it, counsel will see a probability or an improbability, a relationship or a truth which did not occur to him before, and which would not have occurred to him if he had not assembled, perhaps from widely separated sources, the illuminating components. It may not be until the witness has begun to testify that the relevance appears. But whenever it does appear, it may be of great value. It must be remembered that the more obscure a connection or an inference is, the less likely the witnesses are to be ready to deal with it. And it is from the mouth of the unready witness that the truth is most likely to emerge.

As with dates, so with other facts: Even the unattractive looking ducklings which seem to swim on, or slightly outside, the periphery of what is important, should receive some attention. They may turn into swans. This can, perhaps, be most strikingly illustrated by reference to the disputed document—the ledger page which may have been rewritten, or the carbon copy of the letter which, counsel suspects, was never sent. Although the part of the document relevant to the case may be no more than a single entry, or a single sentence, every word, every figure and every punctuation mark in the document deserves study, and comparison with related documents. The paper, the watermark, the ink, or the manner in which the pages of a document have been fastened together may be instructive about authenticity, authorship or date; and the intelligent use of a magnifying glass by counsel may be the first step towards a fruitful examination of the document by an expert.

In a dispute about the conditions of employment of a works manager, the manager alleges that he orally agreed with his employer's managing director that if he was engaged he would be given six weeks' annual leave instead of the normal fortnight. The oral agreement is in dispute, but to support his version the employee produces a carbon copy of a letter which he claims to have handed to the managing director shortly before his engagement. It is a long letter dealing, in the main, with the experience and qualifications of the prospective employee, but in the concluding paragraph the writer refers to an assurance that he will enjoy six weeks' annual leave. The managing director denies that he ever received such a letter.

To counsel, when preparing to cross-examine the employee, it may seem that it is the last paragraph only which deserves his close attention. But that is not so. He must prepare himself fully, in the hope that it may be possible to achieve something like this:

The plaintiff company cannot find any trace of this letter. Did you really send it?

They, or Mr. White, must have lost it.

But they keep a register of every letter received in the office. This would have been entered before it went to Mr. White.

I didn't send it to the office. I handed it to Mr. White personally.

When did you do that?

On the date at the top of the letter.

Are you sure the date is correct?

I can't remember the exact date. I'm sure it was either late in June or early in July, 1962. I don't see why the girl should have typed the wrong date.

Where did you hand Mr. White the letter?

In London. I was there for the day.

Where in London?

At his office, I suppose.

Are you sure?

Pretty sure.

Mr. White was at Wimbledon all that day.

Ah, yes, now I remember. I met him at Wimbledon and gave it to him there. I'd gone to London to see the tennis.

If you were in London for the tennis, how did you come to be writing business letters there?

Mr. White had asked me for a note of my qualifications and experience, to show his Board of Directors, and I went to his office to give it to him on my way to the tennis. He was out,

CROSS-EXAMINATION

so I dictated the letter to a girl in his office, then took it to Wimbledon because they said he was there.

To which girl did you dictate the letter?

Miss Green. The one who later went to Australia.

You had a list of your qualifications. Why was it necessary to have a letter typed?

Well, for one thing, the list had got a bit crumpled in my pocket, and I wanted to make a good impression. For another, I wanted to put the arrangement about leave in writing because it was important to me.

So the list was in your pocket. It's a pretty long list, judging by this carbon copy. Why didn't you carry it in a brief-case?

You don't take a brief-case to the tennis at Wimbledon.

There is nothing to stop you from doing so. Would it not have been worth doing if you had an important document to keep tidy?

Perhaps. But I didn't.

Did you go back to the office before your appointment was confirmed?

No.

Did Miss Green hand you the letter and this carbon copy together?

Yes. I signed the letter and took it and the copy with me to Wimbledon.

In your pocket?

(With a smile)—Yes. But protected against crumpling by an envelope.

The carbon copy was in your pocket?

(The witness hesitates.)

I'm not sure.

You didn't carry it across London in your hand, did you?

No.

How did you carry it?

I suppose in my pocket. I can't really remember.

I hand you the copy. Look at it. Has it been folded?

No. I must have been mistaken. Perhaps I had a brief-case.

GEORGE COLMAN, Q.C.

Which you took to Wimbledon?

It sounds unlikely, but I must have. You yourself have just said that it is possible.

And you said on oath that it had not happened, didn't you?

It's three years ago. It's hard to remember. But it's coming back to me now. I had a newspaper and I slipped the carbon copy into it, flat.

(But this comes too late to carry conviction.)

In the list of your former appointments you refer to one in Zambia.

Yes. In fact I've been back there since, too.

But on the date of this letter there was no country of that name. It was called Northern Rhodesia. How do you explain that?

I'm not so sure you've got your dates right. I'll answer your question when you show me an official document reflecting the date on which the name was changed.

(The witness is struggling for time in which to think.)

Assume that I am right. Can you answer the question?

I can only think it's because I was friendly with a politician in Northern Rhodesia. He told me that its name was going to be Zambia after independence, so I thought of the country by that name.

(This is not impressive.)

And how did you expect Mr. White, who had never been in Africa, to know what country you were referring to?

I was careless.

Did you give Miss Green any instructions about how you wanted the letter typed?

Yes. I said on plain paper, and with one carbon copy.

Anything else?

CROSS-EXAMINATION

What do you mean?

Did you tell her how to set it out, or anything of that sort?

No.

She typed it on her own typewriter?

On the Olivetti in her room.

Can you explain this? The margin on each page of the letter is exactly one inch and a quarter, measured from the edge of the paper.

I suppose that's how Miss Green's typewriter was set.

We have examined ten letters which she typed on the day before the date on this copy, and six typed on the day after. We have examined also a number of other letters which Miss Green typed on other occasions. They all have one and a half inch margins.

You'd better ask Miss Green to explain that.

We have also measured the margins on the two letters the company received from you in June, 1962. Both were typed on an Olivetti and they both bear the initials B.B. Who is B.B.?

My typist, Mrs. Black.

And both letters have a one and a quarter inch margin. Have you any comments to offer?

Yes. I see what you're insinuating. I'll be calling Mrs. Black, and she'll swear that she didn't type this letter which your client is disputing.

So you've asked her. Why?

As soon as your client denied the oral agreement I thought you'd suggest that this letter was a fake, and I showed it to Mrs. Black.

You foresaw the suggestion that the letter was typed in your own office, did you?

Yes. It was obvious that you'd take that line.

It was obvious *to you that my clients would deny receiving a letter which they did receive?*

Yes.

Then why, earlier, did you say that they must have lost it?

It may be appropriate at this stage, to say something for the benefit of the disappointed reader. Of the last example, and of those

GEORGE COLMAN, Q.C.

which went before it, he may say 'But this is not real; it's like cheap detective fiction. The witnesses I have to cross-examine don't make mistakes like these; and if they did, they'd talk their way out of them more intelligently.' To that reader an analysis of the last example may be of some help. But it should be preceded by a reminder of two things which have already been mentioned. The first is that there are many witnesses who cannot be cross-examined successfully, because they are speaking truthfully and accurately of what they know. It has not been thought necessary to give examples of the unsuccessful cross-examination of such witnesses. The second point is that most of the illustrations in this book are not realistic. They bear some such relationship to actual cross-examination as a caricature does to a photograph. What is uninteresting or inessential is omitted; and what is important is exaggerated for the sake of emphasis.

In the last example, counsel will have spent much time on preparation which proved unhelpful. He will have searched the letter for spelling errors and peculiarities of language, but found none that he could use. He has had the paper examined, but found that it was of a type which had been commonly in use for many years. Experts will have told him that the letter was typed on a new typewriter which displayed no idiosyncrasies; and it is not possible to show that the type face of Miss Green's machine was in any way different. He may have caused extensive, but abortive, inquiries to be made about the previous experience of the witness, in the hope of shaking his credibility by pointing to an untruth in the letter.

In court counsel may, in his efforts to show that the carbon copy was a recent fabrication, have attempted several approaches to the witness (e.g. about his motives, his movements and his conduct subsequent to his engagement) which do not appear in the example, because they led nowhere. In his use of the points on which he achieved success, he may not have obtained some of the useful answers as readily as the example suggests; but the intervening thrusts and parries can be imagined.

CROSS-EXAMINATION

That the witness was not mindful of the fact that the copy had not been folded, and did not refrain from giving the damaging answers which counsel linked with that fact, may be explained on the hypothesis that he had been intending to say that he had posted the letter, and that Mr. White must have lost or destroyed it. But when he learnt that there were others in the office who could swear that no such letter had come through the post, he had to improvise, without time for reflection, and he did so clumsily. His damaging statement that he carried no brief-case was made when his attention was focused, not on the letter, but on his original list, and it seemed to him to lend useful support to his invention of a crumpled document; he may have feared, also, that independent witnesses could be found to say that he had no brief-case with him at Wimbledon and, unmindful of the possible consequences, decided, therefore, to say (truthfully) that he had none.

The witness might have taken great care to write the letter as it would have been written on the date it bore; yet, accustomed to using the name Zambia for a country of which he often wrote and spoke, overlooked the fact that that was a new name. He might have been aware that Miss Green used a new typewriter and a type of paper similar to his own; that he overlooked a possible difference in margin settings would not be surprising. His incautious statement about what his own typist would say was made at a time when he knew that he was in trouble. It is not uncommon that a witness thus flustered adds, carelessly, to his mistakes.

The case of the disputed document exemplifies the proper use of what has been styled specific preparation. That type of preparation involves a close study of all that the witness has written, or is known to have said. He may have testified on a previous occasion about the same matter, or a related one, and if he has, counsel should have a record of his evidence and pay attention to every part of it. Having done so, he will, in court, be alert, not only for conflicts, but also for additions and omissions. If the witness is an imaginative one (whether honest or not), he is not unlikely, when testifying for a second time about an event, to remember or think that he remembers, or pretend to remember things which he did not mention on the first occasion. Or, if his evidence on the first occasion was not based on a sound and honest recollection, it may contain improvisations which will not be reproduced when he testifies again. Such divergencies may or may not be significant, but counsel should be ready to use them if they are.

The sort of material referred to, or (if such is not available) counsel's information or belief about the probable content of the evidence which the witness will give, forms the basis of his planning. It is not every cross-examination, even of an expected witness, which can be planned in advance. But some situations call for detailed planning; and in every case it is desirable, if possible, that counsel should formulate some ideas, however sketchy, about the manner in which he may be able to go about his task.

A word here about how not to do it: It is not uncommon for counsel, starting to prepare his first cross-examination, to think of an opening question and to write it down. He then writes down each of the possible answers which he thinks the witness may give, and the questions which he will ask in response to each of these; and so on. There are many reasons for the unworkability of this approach. But the most conclusive one lies in the concept of geometrical progression. There will be neither paper nor time enough to accommodate the overwhelming proliferation of possibilities which the method will produce when applied to a cross-examination of any complication at all. Moreover, it will not be long before the witness comes out with some answer which is not provided for in the scheme, and the cross-examiner will then be lost.

Counsel should never wed himself to a rigidly planned cross-examination. All planning in this craft must be provisional. To what extent the plan will be followed will depend upon what the witness says in chief, how he phrases it, what sort of person he appears to be, and how he responds to questions in cross-examination. Moreover, it is likely that between the planning and the execution the testimony of other witnesses will have been heard; and that may call for modifications in the plan. Counsel must discipline himself, no

CROSS-EXAMINATION

matter how much effort he has put into his planning, to abandon it when that becomes necessary or prudent. He should cultivate in himself not only foresight and industry, but flexibility and the readiness to be opportunistic.

Despite all this, there are situations in which detailed planning is useful, even to the extent that specific questions are carefully formulated in advance. It is often useful so to formulate an opening question. Counsel who is to cross-examine a husband in a matrimonial suit based on desertion or cruelty may not have any clear knowledge about the manner in which he, or the witness, will deal with a long history of married strife. But he may decide that, whatever the witness says in chief, it will probably be useful to open his cross-examination with this question:

Why is your wife, who once loved you, so bitter against you now?

or with this one:

When did you first regret having married your wife?

Elsewhere in this book the reader will find questions, and series of questions, which could well have been formulated in advance.

The most useful type of planning for the cross-examination of a specific witness should follow upon an imaginative effort by counsel. He should visualize himself in the shoes of the witness (as the threadbare metaphor goes) and tread the witness's path through the events relevant to the case, as also through his contemplated cross-examination as it begins to take shape in counsel's mind. At every step counsel should ask himself:

'If his story is true, what would he have done at this stage'?

or

'Why did he do that (or say that)'?

Through this often painful exercise of the imagination counsel may well come upon improbabilities or inconsistencies in the known conduct of the witness, and he will note them as the basis for lines of cross-examination. Or, if no such openings reveal themselves to him, he may think of questions designed to test the conduct and motives of the witness against what could have been expected if his evidence were reliable. From the mental process described there will emerge the raw material of cross-examination in the form of such rough notes as these:

If you really thought he was dishonest, why leave him in charge during May?
Did you report it to the police?
Why didn't you scream?
If you knew all that, why was the item posted to a suspense account?
Had you ever been there before?
(1) What was your financial position then?
(2) Anyone you could have borrowed from?
(3) Wife and how many children?
(4) How could you take the risk?
Did you have a brief-case?
If that was what you thought, why no X-rays?
(1) When first suspect?
(2) What steps taken?

The search is for weaknesses in the version given by the witness, or in the character or reliability of the witness himself. If none are manifest, the search is for methods of exposing them, if they exist.

Much may depend upon counsel's assessment of the witness as deliberately untruthful, honest but confused, imaginative, prejudiced, mistaken, misinformed, ignorant, clever, stupid, subject to pressure, or the like. Sometimes a fair assessment on these matters can be made before the case comes to court; sometimes only when the witness is already testifying; sometimes not at all, in which event flexibility of approach is all important.

CROSS-EXAMINATION

When counsel has resolved upon a few approaches which seem to him to be promising, he should give thorough thought to the order in which he can best put his questions to the witness. He should formulate a provisional policy, for example, as to whether he should open with friendly questions, which the witness can answer easily, in order that a co-operative frame of mind may be built up, or whether it would be wise to hit the witness hard at an early stage, so that he will be conscious of the dangers of untruthfulness. If counsel believes that the witness may be inclined to depart from the truth because the truth will humiliate him in some way, his problem will be to find a method of getting the truth from the witness while saving his face. When he proposes to put a question designed to expose an untruth, he should precede it by others which will close the escape routes which would be open to the witness if the main question were put at once.

In the brief-case example which appears earlier in this chapter, it will be seen that certain questions were put by counsel for the purpose of closing possible escape routes. And on that matter, as on others relevant to the manner in which cross-examination may be prepared, discussions and illustrations will be found in other chapters.

Chapter IV
Material

The term 'material' is used in this chapter to mean anything extrinsic to the evidence of the witness under cross-examination which can be placed before the court, or may legitimately be referred to in cross-examination, and which will or may help to refute, correct, modify or weaken the evidence of the witness, or establish something helpful about the case, or about the witness himself. It includes documents, photographs and material objects; it includes previous statements which the witness has made; and it includes the oral evidence which others have given, or will give, and which, if accepted, may discredit the witness, or otherwise destroy or weaken the effect of what he has said.

The material available to counsel may be strong or weak; it may be conclusive or inconclusive; it may be no more than a remote base from which counsel is driven to attempt an advance into enemy territory. What follows will deal, in the main, with the use of material which, unless carefully handled, will not or may not be conclusive. Counsel who is fortunate enough to command strong, conclusive material, needs no advice about the effective use of it. A prosecutor who is armed with a written confession which is clear in its terms and which has been properly proved, will know how to use it against the efforts of the accused to lie his way out of trouble. The cross-examination of Oscar Wilde by Mr. Edward Carson Q.C. is often cited as an example of forensic skill. But with the material at his command, Carson could hardly have failed.

CROSS-EXAMINATION

When the available material is weak or inconclusive, much depends upon the manner in which it is used. Ably handled, even weak material can have a powerful effect. Clumsily handled, even material which is potentially strong can have but a feeble impact; that is often so when an ingenious and unscrupulous witness has been given full scope for his ingenuity. It should, therefore, be counsel's aim to use his material cautiously, and in the manner appropriate to the circumstances. Here, as always in cross-examination, counsel should consider his case as a whole; and he should strive after an imaginative understanding of the witness—his honesty or otherwise, his temperament, his state of mind, the probable extent of his knowledge, and the degree of mental agility which can be expected of him.

With an honest, intelligent, impartial witness, little or no skill or subtlety is needed in using material. If such a witness, having been a bystander at the scene of a robbery, and having said that the robber looked to him like the accused, has also made other statements about the appearance of the robber, counsel may use his material in this straightforward manner:

Your impression was that the man had a small, dark beard?
Yes.
What if I can prove that the accused never had a beard?
If your proof covers the night of the robbery I'm probably wrong in thinking that the accused was the man.
And the robber was bleeding from the forehead?
Yes, of that I am sure.
What will you say if I tell you that when the accused was seen later that night he had no wound on his forehead?
Then I am certainly wrong.

But with another basically honest witness, so direct an approach may fail, for one reason or another. A common reason is the fear of self-contradiction. It is not unusual for a witness to come to court with the nervous feeling that the object of counsel is to trap him into self-contradiction and that the consequences of that will be grave humiliation or something worse. Such a witness may strive to be consistent at all costs and may be thus impelled either to be stubborn and dogmatic, or to be unnecessarily vague. If, during cross-examination, he finds some measure of self-contradiction unavoidable, he will often try to preserve intact the vital point in his evidence, at any rate; that may be because he feels that it is inconsistency on that point (or what seems to him to be such) which is most likely to expose him to ridicule or other unwanted consequences. The questions used in the last example may, if put to such a witness, evoke these reponses:

> *Your impression was that the man had a small, dark beard; is that not so, Mrs. White?*
> (After a nervous glance at the clean-shaven accused)—Well, it might have been a beard, or a smudge or a shadow.
> *At the time you thought it was a beard, didn't you?*
> I had no time to think.
> I can't say it was a beard. All I can say is that everything else about him looked like the accused.
> *He was bleeding from the forehead, you say?*
> I've told you I had only a glance at him, and the light was not good.
> *But it looked like blood on the forehead; you've said so, haven't you?*
> I did give it as a vague impression. But I shan't let you pin me down. It may not have been blood. Ask the accused. He knows.

This cross-examination has not been entirely fruitless: it has revealed a good deal about the witness. But counsel, with a witness of that kind, might have done better with a different approach. Thus:

> *You have no reason for wishing to harm the accused have you, Mrs. White?*
> None at all.
> *You are here to help the court to the best of your ability, are you not?*

CROSS-EXAMINATION

Yes.

The last thing you want is to have the wrong man convicted?

Yes. But I *would* like to see the right man convicted. And I think the accused is the right man.

You have said 'I think' because you are not sure, and, very properly, you want to avoid misleading the court. Is that right?

Yes.

In fact you are being careful with all your answers because the shock and the bad light prevented you from observing as closely as you would have wished?

Yes. I'm giving my honest impressions, as I remember them.

And, may I take it, after careful reflection?

Yes.

After careful reflection, you were left with the impression that the man had a small, dark beard?

(After a glance at the dock.) That was only an impression.

But you didn't, after careful reflection, suggest the possibility that it was dirt or a mask or anything else. It looked to you like a beard and nothing else. If you'd thought it was anything else you'd have said so, wouldn't you?

Yes.

And the same applies to the blood, doesn't it? After careful reflection, and with a proper wish to assist the court, you said that you saw blood?

Yes.

And the blood was streaming as from a wound in the forehead, was it?

It looked like that. I may have been mistaken.

Anyone in your position could make a mistake. You realize that you could be mistaken in your impression that the man looked like the accused, do you not?

He looked something like the accused.

But if it can be shown that the accused had no beard, and suffered no wound that night, the robber must have been another man who looked something like him. Is that fair?

Yes, I suppose so.

GEORGE COLMAN, Q.C.

The proper use of material in cross-examination often requires an application of the process which has been referred to as 'closing the escape routes'. When a wilfully untruthful witness is to be confronted with material which, on the face of it, appears to contradict him, this is essential. The process is illustrated in the following example. It is a long one, because closing the escape routes, without being too obvious about it, takes time. But it is time well spent.

A plaintiff testifies that a valuable agency was granted to him by the defendant, orally, on the afternoon of 1st March. The defendant will say that there was a discussion about the agency, but no agreement was reached. Counsel is in possession of a letter written by the plaintiff to a creditor of his, dated 1st March, in which he says:

> 'I have news for you which will, I hope, persuade you to be patient. Quite by accident, last night, I got wind of a wonderful opportunity, and I caught the morning plane to London to follow it up. The terms are even more favourable than I hoped, and unless it falls through, the deal should enable me to pay you in full within a year or less. ... '

This is a useful piece of material. But if it is used incautiously, the plaintiff may be able to explain it away. (He is, by hypothesis, an untruthful witness.) It occurs to counsel that he may say that the 'deal' referred to in the letter was not the agency agreement, but some transaction with another person in London, which was never concluded. Or he may say that it was another transaction discussed with the defendant, and left open when the agency agreement was concluded. Another possibility is that he will say that, when he referred to the deal falling through, he had in mind that the defendant might dishonestly deny or break the agreement. If the witness remembers the terms of the letter, and has seen their implications, he may be ready with a story which cannot be broken down. But as the case is a complicated one, involving many documents, counsel hopes that the witness, with many other things on

CROSS-EXAMINATION

his mind, will not be so well prepared. He tries to close the escape routes:

Is your memory clear about your interview with the defendant?
Yes.
Have you a good memory for detail?
Pretty good, I think.
Do you remember the other events of that day?
I think so.

(Counsel's intention is that, when answering the following questions, the witness will be thinking not of the letter, but of the display of memory which he is giving. Without this introduction the witness will be more likely to see where the questions are leading.)

How long were you with the defendant?
For about an hour.
At what time?
I'd say from three to four in the afternoon.
At what time did you reach London?
11.15.
What did you do with the rest of the time?
spent most of the time till lunch trying to get the defendant on the phone. I must have put through six calls.
From where?
The Hyde Park Hotel.
Did you telephone anyone else?
No.
Had you no other appointments to make?
No.
You came to London to see the defendant and for no other purpose?
I thought of visiting my tailor, and I did. But that was incidental.
Did you have any business discussions with anyone at all before you went to the defendant?
No. Unless you call ordering a couple of suits a business discussion.

GEORGE COLMAN, Q.C.

What did you discuss with the defendant?

The Star Agency, the weather, the budget.

Anything else?

Not that I remember. I remember essentials more easily than details.

You discussed no transaction or deal with him other than the Star Agency?

No.

Was the agency important to you?

It was vital.

Why didn't you put the agreement into writing?

We were both pressed for time and I trusted him.

But you didn't know him, did you?

He seemed honest. And I'd made inquiries about him at home. He had a good reputation. But for that I would not have dealt with him.

You and he reached a firm and final agreement?

Firm, final and binding.

Was it not contingent upon anything at all?

On nothing.

Was there nothing which might have made it impossible to carry it into effect?

The supplies were there ... transport was available. ... My answer is: nothing except rank dishonesty on the defendant's part. But, as I say, nothing was further from my mind than that.

When did you first suspect that he might deny the agreement, or try to back out of it?

Never. His denial in June was a shock to me.

Until then, were you confident that you had the agency and would profit from it?

I had no doubt on either point.

You say that on the day of the agreement you were pressed for time?

After the agreement, yes.

Why?

I had a call to make before flying home.

On whom?

What's this all about? It has nothing to do with the case.

CROSS-EXAMINATION

On whom?

A friend.

A business friend?

No. A lady, if you must know.

I have no interest in your private affairs, but tell me this: Did you discuss business with the lady?

No.

Did either of you refer, directly or indirectly, to the agency or to the defendant?

No.

Was there any such reference between you and anyone at all after you left the defendant?

If you mean that day, the answer is no … wait. … If you mean in conversation, the answer is no.

After leaving the defendant, did you talk to anyone at all, apart from the lady, before you got home?

A taxi-driver—two taxi-drivers. That's all.

Did you receive any written communication from anyone in London that day?

No.

What did you do on the aircraft?

I wrote a few letters.

Where did you post them?

On the airport after we touched down.

Was one of them to your creditor White?

Yes.

The witness may yet find some method of explaining the letter away. But not so easily as if counsel had left the obvious escape routes open.

Here is counsel closing two escape routes before making use of a piece of tangible material. The accused, when arrested on a charge of housebreaking and theft, was wearing a leather belt. The victim has said that among the things stolen was a belt, and that he thinks that the one found on the accused is that belt. The accused, in evidence, says that he bought the belt at a shop months before the robbery. The accused is a slim man; the victim of the robbery is a good deal stouter, and prosecuting counsel notices, on the surface of the belt, not one, but two wear marks manifestly made by the edge of the buckle while the belt was in use. They are several inches apart, and with the buckle against one of them the belt would be far too large for the accused. Before drawing attention to this, counsel asks:

For what purpose did you buy the belt?
What do you think? To keep my trousers up.
Some men manage to keep their trousers up without belts, don't they?
Not I. My hips are narrow.
So you have always worn a belt?
Yes.
Every day?
Yes.
Then I take it you already had a belt when you bought this one. Did you?
Yes, but it was getting very shabby.
What did you do with the old belt?
I gave it to my son.
Did you, then, wear this belt every day from the day you bought it till the day of your arrest?
Yes.
Every day, without exception? Were you never ill in bed?
No. My health is good.
Did you never lend the belt to anyone?
No.
And as your health was good, can I take it that you haven't gained or lost weight since you bought the belt?

(The witness now begins to see what is coming.)

May I see the belt, please?
Not at this stage. Did you lose or gain weight?

CROSS-EXAMINATION

Yes. For the last six months before my arrest I was dieting.

Why did you want to see the belt before telling me that?

I thought I might be able to show you marks on the belt to prove that I'd been dieting. I'm not sure they're there. I haven't seen the belt since my arrest. But they may be.

Here is the belt. Are there such marks?

Yes, here, and here.

You have shown me a mark near the second hole in the belt, and another mark near the eighth hole. Do they represent your waist before and after dieting?

It must be so. Otherwise you wouldn't find the two marks.

There are no marks between those two. Tell me please, what diet is it which shrunk your waistline about six inches so suddenly that at no stage did you buckle your belt on any hole between the second and the eighth?

In the next illustration, what seems to be a very weak piece of material, produces dramatic success with an honest witness:

So you see, doctor, the radiologist advising me interprets the X-ray plate quite differently from you?

I'm surprised, but I can't help it. Here the plate is, and it speaks clearly to me.

Are you incapable of misreading a plate?

Not this one.

If I show you that you have misread it in any respect at all, will that surprise you?

Yes.

Today you have said that the kneecap was broken into seven pieces. In your preliminary report last April I find this phrase: 'The eight fragments of the patella.' It may be a minor point; but you did misread the plate, then or now, did you not?

It is a minor point. And it was a hasty report. You will notice that it contains no conclusions. But I shouldn't have made such a mistake. Let me see.... Good heavens, I've been looking at the wrong plate!

If he is to make effective use of his material, counsel must be clear in his own mind about the result which he is hoping to achieve. This statement is not intended to detract from what has been said earlier about the multiple aims of cross-examination. In the use of material, as elsewhere, counsel will sometimes frame his questions with alternative possibilities in mind. But he should be conscious of each of those possibilities, and, generally speaking, he should know which of the possible results he would prefer.

When the material is a prior statement by the witness, or a statement which someone else has made, or will make, counsel's primary wish may be to get confirmation of that statement from the witness. In such a case it will usually be wise to put the material to the witness before inviting him to make any statement which might conflict with it. If that is not done, the witness, having said something in conflict with the material, may adhere to his answer and try to explain the material away.

If, on the other hand, the primary aim is to discredit the witness, counsel should draw him out on the point covered by the material before using it.

When you joined the firm, did you think that conditions in the building industry would soon improve?
I hoped so, but I feared that they would not.
Why?
The municipal figures showed a drop. And the rise in interest rates wasn't going to help.
May I suggest to you that municipal figures are a deceptive index.
I regard them as significant.
Did you so regard them then?
I certainly did.
But wasn't there still plenty of money about—money for investment in office blocks?
I don't think so. Not at that time.
You'll not go so far as to say that you were gloomy about the industry, will you?

CROSS-EXAMINATION

On a long-term basis, no. About the short-term prospects I was pessimistic.

How long is the short term?

I thought it would take three years, at least, before we'd see a recovery.

Do you remember what you said to the Chamber of Commerce two days before you joined the firm?

No. But I must tell you we try to look on the bright side there.

To the extent that you say the opposite of what you mean?

Not to that extent, no.

Mr. White, who was present, will tell the court that you expressed great optimism about the immediate prospects for the industry.

Mr. White is the plaintiff's brother-in-law.

Do you suggest that his evidence will be false?

If he says that he'll be lying.

Those are strong words. Are you sure your memory is not deceiving you?

I remember my state of mind vividly. And I'll add this: If I'd been happy about the short-term prospects of the building industry I'd never have joined the firm.

So anyone who tells the court that you said 'there is every cause for great optimism about the immediate future of the building industry' is not telling the truth?

If Mr. White says I used those words, he is lying.

You know Mr. Black, the accountant, don't you?

Yes.

He is not the plaintiff's brother-in-law, is he?

No.

Can you suggest any reason at all why he should lie about you?

No. But he may be confusing me with someone else.

He was so impressed with your views that he made a note of them at the time, which he will show the court, if necessary. It is headed with your name, and the words which I quoted appear in it. He has also noted your remark that 'municipal figures are a highly deceptive index'. What do you say now?

GEORGE COLMAN, Q.C.

It should be noticed how counsel kept his best material (Mr. Black's note) in reserve until the witness had committed himself fully. The reference to Mr. White was introduced deliberately to invite a strong denial which could later be proved false. It will be seen, also, that at an early stage counsel introduced the expression 'deceptive index' as if it were his own. Such a use of the witness's own words, if he is likely to have forgotten them, can be highly effective.

A somewhat different method of using material is called for when counsel is not content, thereby, to refute what the witness has said, and has prospects, in addition, of demonstrating the extent to which the witness, deliberately or unconsciously, can distort facts or exaggerate. Here, again, success may be possible only when the witness is unaware of the material, or has forgotten or failed to realize its implications. But that happens more frequently than a person without experience of litigation might suspect. An untruthful witness, in particular, often has so much to think about and guard against, both before he comes to court and during his testimony, that he overlooks things.

The object of the cross-examiner, in the case under discussion, is to reveal the unreliability of the witness by getting him to commit himself to statements so far in conflict with the material later to be placed before the court that he is fully discredited. A by-product of the process may be that the witness, if he is honest, though irresponsible, will, when confronted with the material, be shocked into dealing more circumspectly with subsequent questions put to him. If he is a rogue, the revelation may fluster him to the extent that he will fare badly under further cross-examination. He may, on the other hand, be shocked into a greater alertness; that is a risk which counsel must take.

A colonial governor finds, outside his residency, a mass gathering of the local population, demanding that he discuss their grievances with them. He is unwilling to do that, and orders them to leave. When they persist in disobeying such orders, he causes the residency guards to open fire on the crowd, and at a subsequent inquiry he gives evidence in justification of the shooting, which,

CROSS-EXAMINATION

he claims, was necessary in defence of himself and his family. Counsel, who cross-examines him, has some photographs of the scene, taken by a newspaperman; before producing them, he cross-examines thus:

But why didn't you talk to them?
I wasn't going to show weakness. It would have been most unwise.
But surely a little loss of dignity by you was preferable to a cold blooded killing?
The killing was not cold-blooded. If there had been any alternative I'd have taken it.
One alternative was to talk to them, was it not?
I'd have had a knife in my back before I got far with the talking.
You were afraid, governor?
You don't seem to realize that I was dealing with an angry crowd.
Very angry?
Very angry indeed.
How do you know they were very angry? You didn't talk to them. Perhaps they could have been calmed down.
I've had plenty of experience with crowds. I know a frenzied mob when I see one.
Was this a frenzied mob?
Indeed it was. They were shouting, waving sticks and knives, and they had murderous looks on their faces. They were out for blood.
What, all of them?
Most of them.
I suggest to you that there was an angry group of young men on the south-east corner, but the rest of the crowd was peaceful?
That is wrong.
You saw a frenzied mob on all three sides of the building?
Yes.
Most of them armed?
Yes.
Angry beyond control?

GEORGE COLMAN, Q.C.

Yes.

Was it not your duty to calm them down?

That was impossible. They'd come there thirsting for blood. If I hadn't opened fire I wouldn't be alive today. Nor would my guards be.

Were they in that mood throughout?

Yes.

From the moment they arrived until the shooting they looked and behaved as you have described?

Yes. If they'd shown any signs of calming down I'd have tried to talk to them.

Here is a photograph of a section of the crowd on the south-west. Can you show me a murderous look on any of the faces?

They may not look so to you, but I know these people. Look at that one—there's a nasty glint in his eye.

Where are the weapons?

Concealed, I suppose. They're crafty people.

So it was concealed weapons, was it, which seemed to you to be the threat?

Partly.

Here is a photograph of the main body of the crowd. How many weapons do you see?

There are two sticks. And it looks as if that man has a knife.

Is that all?

All I can point to.

There are many small children here. Do these people take their babies with them to a murderous attack on a building defended by soldiers?

Apparently.

Look carefully at those photographs, and the third one which I hand you. Look at the two young girls with parasols. Look at the old woman holding a cat. Look at the four men lounging on the pavement. And look at one of your own guards looking over the fence and laughing at your frenzied, murderous mob. Is it a frenzied, murderous mob?

The pictures, somehow, don't convey the atmosphere.

CROSS-EXAMINATION

*Look at the woman pushing the perambulator. Is she pushing her infant
into a frenzied mob?*

I've answered that.

*The boy eating the banana and the two men reading the newspaper are
members of a frenzied mob, are they?*

I didn't say every person there was in a frenzy.

*But none of these people seem to have noticed that they are in the middle
of a murderous, frenzied mob, do they?*

I can't answer for them.

Your guards were very brave men, were they not?

Yes.

*So brave that, when facing the prospect of being murdered by a frenzied
mob, some of them were lounging against a fence and laughing?*

What if the photographs had been less conclusive? What if the
only significant point in them had been the relaxed attitudes of
some of the guards? In that event counsel would have built up to his
point more cautiously:

You are no coward, are you?

I trust not.

*What was your state of mind during the few minutes before shooting?
Panic?*

I did not panic.

In spite of the imminent danger to yourself and your men?

No. I was under strain, but clear-headed.

Would you say that your guards were under strain?

I can speak only for myself.

*Was it you alone who could see the dangers? Are your men incapable of
recognizing a frenzied mob?*

That is an absurd suggestion.

It must have been plain to your men that they were in grave danger?

Yes, it was obvious.

*Grave and immediate danger? Yes. Look at this photograph. Look at your
guards.*

GEORGE COLMAN, Q.C.

What counsel will do with his material, if he can, is to create a dilemma for the witness, in the sense that the witness is driven to give one of two answers, either of which will be damaging to the litigant for whom he is testifying. It may be that each horn of the dilemma is a statement of fact directly adverse to the litigant on an issue in the case. Or it may be that the witness has to choose between a statement adverse to the case and a statement adverse to his own character or credibility. Thus:

> *What you said in this letter was either true or false. Either the machine was working properly, or you were concealing from your employer what you had no right to conceal. Which was it?*

or

> *Your brake marks were only eleven feet long. Is that because you didn't see the cycle until you were past the post office, or because you saw him but didn't apply your brakes until it was too late?*

In each of these examples the two horns of the dilemma have, for the sake of brevity, been dealt with in one question. Although such a question is often appropriate, counsel will more frequently find it better to cross-examine first on one horn, and thus drive the witness on to the other. Normally, though not invariably, he would be well advised to put his questions first on the alternative, rather than the one which he would prefer to establish.

A device favoured by some counsel which, perhaps, falls within the ambit of this chapter, is to confront the witness with the person who will contradict his evidence, by bringing that person into the courtroom, or making him stand up. In the experience of the writer, this is of doubtful utility, except in special circumstances. If there is reason to think that the witness does not believe that the conflicting testimony is available, the production of the person who will give it may have useful results, although often such production should be deferred until the witness has had every opportunity of

CROSS-EXAMINATION

saying things which he might have hesitated to say if he had known that there was someone to contradict him. And it may be that the production of a young, beautiful and angelic-looking stranger will make a witness hesitate to deny what he is told that she will swear to. Ordinarily, however, the confrontation is unlikely to have any useful effects.

The emphasis, in this chapter, has been on material which bears upon the merits of the dispute. But counsel sometimes has available to him material which bears solely upon the character or reliability of the witness. Such material can be of great value, but its use presents this special problem: Although the law of evidence permits counsel to cross-examine as to credit, and in so doing, to put facts to a witness, he may not, on a point relevant solely to credibility, lead evidence to contradict what the witness has said. Such contradiction is permitted, on the other hand, if the evidence, though primarily important because of its effect on credibility, can fairly be said also to have a relevance to one of the issues in the case. In certain cases the law may regard the character of some witnesses as being in issue; but those are exceptional cases.

A consequence of the rule of evidence is that in an ordinary case a witness who is sufficiently unscrupulous, and who knows the rule, can deny a proposition which he knows to be true, if it bears solely upon his character, without fear that evidence will be led to contradict him. But comparatively few witnesses know the rule; and even fewer are able to distinguish clearly between what relates solely to credibility and what is otherwise relevant. Moreover, despite the rule, a witness who lies on a matter relating to credit will be liable to prosecution for perjury. And in such a prosecution he can be faced with evidence to prove that what he said was false.

For these reasons counsel who has material relating only to the character or credibility of a witness will often be able to extract from the witness himself the information which he wishes the court to have. If he asks his questions firmly, and in a manner which suggests that he knows the facts, the witness will not find it easy to lie about them.

GEORGE COLMAN, Q.C.

In a case where counsel fears that the witness knows of the rule, and is likely to give untruthful answers because he knows that, in this suit, at any rate, he cannot be contradicted, counsel will adopt this course, if the circumstances permit it: he will try, by suitable cross-examination, to render the matter relevant not only to credibility, but also to one of the issues. If he succeeds in doing that, the rule of evidence will lay the witness open to contradiction; and the witness may be induced to be truthful by the knowledge that counsel will not be bound by his answers.

The owner-editor of a magazine is under cross-examination in a case relating to some untruthful matter which he has written and published about the plaintiff. The witness claims that before publication he checked the information available to him carefully, and that he published in good faith. Whether he did so or not, is relevant to an issue in the case. Counsel has information that on two previous occasions, the witness, when working for other publications, had recklessly written false reports. This, if it can be established, is likely to affect credibility. But counsel, fearing that the witness may brazenly deny the previous incidents, lays his foundation thus:

What made you take such care before publishing?
I should think the answer would be obvious. I didn't want to be
    sued for damages.
Was that the only reason?
I didn't say it was the only reason.
You were your own master. Apart from a claim for damages, what had
    you to fear?
I had my reputation as a journalist to think of.
You thought of that?
Of course. Mine is as honourable a profession as yours.
Are you seriously suggesting that at the time when you were about to write
    this article you had your journalistic reputation in mind?
Indeed I had. I'm still a young man. I may be looking for a post
    on one of the big papers some day.

CROSS-EXAMINATION

Would a reputation for irresponsibility handicap you in getting such a post?

Yes. I've told you; journalism is an honourable profession.

And you regard yourself as an honourable and responsible member of that profession?

I do.

And when you were preparing to write this article you had it consciously in mind that unless you were careful, your good name as an honest and responsible journalist might suffer?

I did.

You didn't expect this publication to improve your reputation in that regard, did you?

I think I said protect, not improve. I wrote the article to expose a scandal, not to advance my own interests.

The foundation has been laid. Counsel continues:

Let us examine the good name which you were seeking to protect. What work were you doing in the six months before you started this magazine?

I was looking round for an opening. And when I found one, I was arranging to start the magazine.

During that period, did you apply for any jobs?

One or two ... perhaps three.

You didn't get them, obviously. Can you tell me why?

They didn't say why.

Have you no idea why, because if you haven't, I'm going to suggest one to you?

It may have had something to do with my job on the 'News'.

You lost that job, didn't you?

Yes. Unjustly, for an error of judgment.

We won't go into the justice of it at the moment. But did that error of judgment, as you call it, lead to the publication of an untrue statement for which the paper had to pay heavy damages?

Yes, I suppose you could call them heavy.

GEORGE COLMAN, Q.C.

And the error of judgment lay in saying that a lady had been found guilty of theft when she hadn't. You didn't bother to find out the result of the case, before writing your report, did you?

I don't like 'didn't bother'. Everybody was sure she was going to be found guilty, and it never entered my mind that the result would be different. I still don't know what was in the jury's mind.

Two years ago, I think, you had trouble of a similar nature.

I suppose you mean my editorial about the Black Engineering Company. I wouldn't call that similar. For one thing no damages were paid.

You published an apology?

Yes. The Black Engineering Company's lawyers drafted it.

Maybe; but you signed it. And in it you said: 'I concede that the imputation against the company was untrue and groundless, and that with proper care I could have ascertained that without difficulty.' May I take it that, as a member of an honourable profession, you would not have published an apology in those terms unless it was accurate?

It was strongly worded.

Was it inaccurate?

No.

Is it not fair, then, to say that at the time we are concerned with, you had no good name as a responsible and careful journalist to protect?

CHAPTER V
UNARMED COMBAT

This chapter deals with a situation which differs from that in the immediately preceding one, in that counsel approaches his task unaided by any material. There are no documents which conflict with what the witness is deposing to; there are no tangible objects to contradict or throw doubt on his evidence in chief; and there are no other witnesses who will contradict him, or none whose evidence will necessarily be accepted in preference to his; counsel has nothing upon which to attack the character of the witness, and nothing which proves that he is biased. Yet it is necessary to destroy or weaken the testimony of the witness, if that is possible by legitimate means. It will be assumed, in order that this chapter may be kept to a suitable length, that the witnesses referred to therein are deliberately untruthful. Honest witnesses will be discussed elsewhere.

Counsel's task, in the situation postulated, is to create his material out of the witness's own mouth; and in order to do that, he will have to be alert for weaknesses both in the substance of the testimony and in the manner in which it is given.

There are, undoubtedly, some people who are capable of lying with every appearance of honesty and candour. But, happily, it is not every untruthful witness who commands that gift. Often there is something to be learnt from a close observation of demeanour; counsel should, therefore, watch and listen for significant signs which may appear at any stage during evidence in chief or cross-examination. A difficulty which sometimes arises is that counsel

GEORGE COLMAN, Q.C.

wishes, during the evidence in chief, to make notes of what the witness is saying; and, indeed, such notes are often useful and sometimes necessary. But if counsel is to note fully the whole of the evidence in chief, he may miss much that would be useful to him. He should form the habit, therefore, of noting only what cannot be remembered, and that as briefly as possible. If his concentration upon what the witness says is intense enough, his memory, aided by a few jottings, should serve his purpose.

Counsel's concentration on the subject-matter of the evidence should be combined with close attention to the manner in which it is presented. He should watch the witness as he would watch a conjurer whose methods he was trying to detect—interested in what is emphasized, but equally interested in what is unemphasized, omitted, or slurred. There may be some section or detail of his evidence which the witness presents more hurriedly, or with less assurance than the rest, or perhaps, with more deliberation. There may be, somewhere, an unusually long pause, a hesitation, the drawing of a deep breath. The witness may be seen to swallow hard; he may change his tone, or he may take a hurried glance at someone other than the person who is questioning him. Counsel may notice some nervous gesture with a hand or a shoulder which appears at certain stages.

Such manifestations, during cross-examination or evidence in chief, may or may not be significant. It is not every nervous witness who is untruthful. But a hesitation, an over-boldness, a sign of discomfort, may be the pointer to an important weakness, and the cross-examiner should take notice of the point at which it occurs, particularly if it is not the central or most dramatic point in the evidence. If a mother is describing how she saw a hit-and-run motorist knock her child over, it will not be surprising or significant that she shows signs of distress when she comes to speak of the impact. But, it may well be significant if, when asked what colour the car was, she hesitates, looks round the room, and then says, in a lower tone than she has been using, 'Blue'. Counsel will note this conduct and, perhaps, decide to open his cross-examination on the colour of the

CROSS-EXAMINATION

car. There are many ways in which he could do that. One would be to look hard at the witness and say, very slowly, firmly and clearly—

Think carefully before you answer; are you absolutely certain that the car which struck your child was blue?

If this question, and the manner in which it is put, give the witness the impression that counsel perhaps knows more than she thought, she may at once make a confession of uncertainty. If she does not, counsel may continue—

Have you ever had the slightest doubt that it was blue?
No.
You know now, don't you, that the defendant's car is blue?
I've been told so.
What else have you been told about the defendant's car?

Details are given and, if necessary, clarified by means of further questioning. Then:

Before you were told the colour of the defendant's car, were you absolutely certain that it was a blue car which hit your child?
Yes, I was.
You have never had the slightest doubt about it?
No.
Did you ever express any doubt about it to anyone?
No.
Then why did you hesitate when asked about it during your evidence in chief?
Did I? I don't know why.

Counsel may then go on to ask about other features of the car, to many of which the witness will reply that she did not notice, or is not sure. He may then point out to her that this is not surprising, because she only caught a momentary glimpse of the car before the impact. If she accepts that:

GEORGE COLMAN, Q.C.

And your attention was fixed on your child, wasn't it?

Yes.

You were horrified?

Yes, I was almost paralysed with fright.

You were in no state to concentrate on the details of the car, were you?

No, but I saw it as it hit my child.

After the impact, you kept your eyes on the child, not on the car, didn't you?

Yes.

So all you had was a momentary glimpse of a car rushing at your child. And your attention was on the child?

Yes.

It's very hard to be sure of the colour in those circumstances, I suggest to you—so sure that you can swear to it.

All I can say is it looked blue to me.

It looked blue; did it look dark blue?

No, lightish blue.

Could it have been greenish-blue?

It could have been.

Could it have been light green?

I suppose it could have been.

A witness who has been answering questions under cross-examination in a relaxed, informal manner, changes his tone when asked:

Did you, during January, hear that the plaintiff was in financial difficulty?

He responds, slowly and carefully.

No. I did not hear that he was in financial difficulty.

If counsel notices the change of tone, and the precise manner in which the answer is framed, his next question will be:

CROSS-EXAMINATION

What did *you hear about him?*

And the witness may, either at once, or after the point has been pressed, say:

Well, someone did tell me that he'd sold his wife's diamonds.

Counsel may suspect that the evidence in chief, or some part of it, has been learnt by heart. This often happens with children, and sometimes with simple adults. That a witness has learnt by heart something to which he knows that he will have to speak in evidence, does not necessarily mean that he is untruthful. A nervous witness, or a very conscientious one, might do that even if his evidence is entirely true. But untruthful witnesses often do it; and so do witnesses who, while not wholly untruthful, have not such a clear recollection of the subject-matter of their testimony as they are trying to suggest. It is therefore desirable that, if possible, it be revealed to the court that the evidence has been learnt by heart.

In an effort to do that, counsel will ask the witness to repeat certain parts of the evidence in chief, and if that is done in the same words as were originally used, it may be significant. Some witnesses will even reproduce, strikingly, their original intonations. Counsel will (after diverting the attention of the witness to other matters, if possible) revert to the matter which appears to have been learnt by rote; but this time he will depart from the natural sequence of events. He will ask, in an order which is neither chronological, nor logical, a series of questions directed to specific details covered by the evidence in chief. From the answers to these, it is likely to become clear, if that is the case, that the witness has not been drawing upon a true recollection of the events about which he speaks, but has been reciting something which he has learnt.

It is not only when something appears to have been learnt by heart that there is value in the device of turning, in haphazard order, from one detail to another. A fabricated story is easier to tell plausibly when the recital follows a preconceived order or plan; improbabilities, inconsistencies and other weaknesses are more likely to appear when counsel exercises his privilege of darting back and forth among the details of the narrative.

Another opening which counsel should be ready to exploit will appear when the witness seems to be trying to avoid giving a direct answer to some question. Even if the point does not appear to counsel to be an important one, he should insist upon the direct answer. The witness may have some reason for his evasion, and that reason might have a bearing on the case. The answer may, for example, reveal an unsuspected motive for untruthfulness. In the following example a witness who was, on the face of it, an independent eye-witness to an accident, is shown to have a connection with one of the parties to the suit, and thus a possible motive for lying. At the same time a lack of candour is revealed:

A few moments ago you spoke of the plaintiff by his first name, as if you knew him. Did you know him before the accident.
His full name is on the notice board outside this court. And I think I heard you yourself refer to him as Mr. Arthur Green.
I asked you whether you knew him before the accident.
I have told the court what I saw. It wouldn't have made any difference whether I knew him or not.
But did you know him?
I'd seen him.
Where?
Oh, in a couple of places. Mainly at his office.
Why did you go to his office?
To do some typing.
Were you employed there?
Yes—but we weren't very close friends.
Why didn't you say at once that you and Mr. Green had worked together?

Counsel cannot, of course, be confident that such opportunities as these will present themselves. His main search for a promising opening will be in the content of the evidence itself. He will bring the full force of his imagination to bear on the story which the

CROSS-EXAMINATION

witness tells, and he will be constantly asking himself such questions as these about the witness:

How did he come to be there?
What was he doing?
How much would he have seen, heard, noticed?
Why does she remember that?
What would she have done if that really happened?
Whom would she have told?
How did they find him?
Why should he lie?
How does she know that?
How will it affect him if I lose this case?—How if I win it?

Some of these, he may decide, are questions which he should put directly to the witness. It would be hard to think of a more useful question than:

What makes you remember that so clearly?

Some events, of course, are so important to a litigant that he would not forget them. Others are so striking that even a person not directly concerned will remember them. In relation to these the question will not be put. But the perjurer sometimes claims to recollect things which would not ordinarily be remembered. And that standby of the dishonest litigant, the apparently disinterested stranger, is often hard put to it to explain why he happens to remember details which, though never of any importance to him, are so valuable to the party who has called him.

Unless the event deposed to has some inherent interest, the witness may feel driven to invent some reason for remembering it, and that, competently handled by the cross-examiner, may be revealing:

The defendant often came to buy cigarettes at your shop, didn't he?

He'd drop in for a packet two or three times a week.

Like many other business men in the neighbourhood?

Yes.

Was your relationship with him any different from your relationship with any other customer?

I don't know what you mean by relationship. He came and bought cigarettes and left.

How is it that you remember that on that particular afternoon he was wearing a grey overcoat?

I just happen to remember. It was the only time he wore that coat.

But how can you distinguish that afternoon from any other afternoon on which he came in?

Well, that was the day on which his house burnt down.

But you didn't hear of that until weeks later, did you?

A couple of weeks—when the attorney came to ask me about it.

How were you then able to remember what he wore on that particular day?

It was a cold day.

It was a cold fortnight, Mrs. Brown. What did he wear the next time he came in?

Some other coat. I'm not sure of the colour.

And the previous time he came in? I don't know. *You have no idea?*

I think it was a black coat.

And if I tell you he has never owned or worn a black coat?

Well, I may be wrong. I said I *thought* it was black.

You see Mr. White here in court. He also visited your shop that day. Can you tell me what coat he wore?

A brown one, I'd say.

Brown?

Did you say brown?

I don't really know. It was a long time ago.

It was indeed a long time ago. Are you sure that Mr. White was wearing a coat at all?

I can't swear to it.

CROSS-EXAMINATION

But you can *swear that the defendant wore a grey coat! You saw the defendant here in court yesterday. What were the colours of his suit and tie?*

I think it was a dark suit. I really can't say about his tie.

You don't seem to be very observant. Why do you remember that on an afternoon over a year ago the defendant wore a grey overcoat? Can you give the court no explanation?

(The witness, feeling the weakness of her position, now improvises.)

I remember mentioning it to my sister who came in soon afterwards.

What made you mention it to her?

I was telling her about a new skirt which I'd bought the previous day. It was the same colour as the defendant's coat.

Why didn't you mention that before?

It's just come back to me.

What was the point in telling her that the skirt was the same colour as a coat she had never seen?

It just came in, somehow. How do you expect me to remember such trifles?

I'll ask you about something less trifling. Where had you bought your skirt the previous day?

At one of the big shops.

You can't remember which shop? Is your memory as bad as all that?

I didn't say I couldn't remember. It was at Modern Modes, in Main Street. I buy nearly all my clothes there.

You have an account there?

Yes.

(The following day.)

We have been in touch with Modern Modes. They say that you bought only one skirt from them last year. Is that right?

If they say so.

And it was a green skirt, is that right?

I don't think their records will show the colour. I looked at a green skirt, but I bought a grey one. Whoever you spoke to is confused.

Maybe. But their records do show the date. And it was three weeks after the fire that you bought the skirt. Can you dispute that? Would you like to see a copy of the slip you signed?

I must have made a mistake about the skirt.

Then I'll ask you again: How do you remember that the defendant was wearing a grey coat on that particular afternoon?

A witness often claims to be able to remember an event because he made a note of it at the time; and he may, even if his evidence is wholly false, be ready to produce a document which cannot be shown to have been made recently, even if in fact it was. But that will sometimes open up a useful line of inquiry about the reason for making the note.

Miss Black, have you any interest in this divorce case between your neighbours?

I couldn't care less.

You have referred twice to the quarrel in the garden which you say you overheard, and on both occasions you gave the exact words. How do you remember them so precisely?

I made a note of them.

In order to be able to quote them accurately in this case?

No. It was long before I knew that there would be a case.

Did you not think that there might be one?

It never entered my mind.

When did you last look at your note?

About an hour ago. Just before I was called.

Let me see it please. ... Thank you. ... Now if you didn't expect to be a witness, and had no interest in these people's quarrels, why did you make a note of what they said to each other?

I've always wanted to write a novel, and I thought that I might use this as material.

Was that your only reason for making the note?
Yes.
Then why did you head your note with the date, the time, and the address?

Of a witness who claims to be completely independent, and a stranger to the interested parties, it is sometimes fruitful to inquire how he comes to be a witness. Thus, to the lady in the previous example, the following questions might be put:

Having made the note for the purposes of your novel, did you tell anyone about it, or its contents?
No.
Did you not, perhaps, discuss it with the plaintiff, or at any rate tell her that you had overheard her husband's abusive language to her?
No. I've never spoken to her in my life.
Then how did she or her attorney know that you were able to give evidence in this case?

The question 'Have you discussed this with anyone?' is part of the seasoned cross-examiner's regular stock-in-trade. A surprising number of litigants and witnesses appear to believe that any previous discussion with anyone of the subject-matter of their testimony is in some way discreditable, or is likely to make their evidence suspect. Some of them will, therefore, firmly deny previous discussion even in circumstances when it must have taken place. It is not unknown, even, for a witness to deny that he has had any communication with the litigant who has called him, or anyone representing that litigant: that witness may find himself in grave difficulty when asked to explain how he came to be called as a witness.

When such a disavowal of previous discussion is plainly untrue, it reflects adversely on the credibility of the witness. But this particular falsehood is so common, even in the mouths of otherwise satisfactory witnesses, that many courts hesitate to attach great importance to it.

Another question which is sometimes useful when put to an untruthful witness is:

But why should these witnesses, who have no interest in this case, lie about you?

The witness may feel that he has to invent reasons, and when he does, they may well be implausible reasons, which can lead him into difficulties during further questioning; or they may be reasons which can be proved, by other evidence, to be untrue.

Perhaps the capacity most useful to counsel who has to cross-examine without material is an imagination vivid enough to enable him to put himself, notionally, into the situation which the witness claims to have occupied, and to see clearly how the witness would have acted if his or her account had been true. Thus, to the employee who has given a long recital of unjust treatment at the hands of his immediate superior:

But how are you able to remember all these details covering a period of eighteen months?
I made notes of them.
Why?
Because I realized that he was trying to get me out of the firm.
So eighteen months before you were actually dismissed you saw it coming?
I did. It had been going on for some time before that.
You felt, eighteen months before your dismissal, that Mr. Brown was deliberately and maliciously forcing you into an intolerable position?
I knew it, and I decided to fight back.
About a year before your dismissal you went to see the managing director about your insurance payments, didn't you?
Yes.
Why didn't you tell him about the persecution?
I didn't know him well enough.

Cross-Examination

But your position was becoming desperate, and you'd decided to fight back. Why not fight back by complaining to the managing director?

I thought he'd take Mr. Brown's side.

But this was your one chance, was it not? Why didn't you try?

Perhaps I was wrong, but I thought it was hopeless.

So you just carried on, with the feeling that at any time you might be dismissed, or forced to resign?

Yes. I decided to hang on as long as possible. I have five children to support.

I see. Now obviously, a man in that unhappy position would have been making applications for other jobs. May I see copies of your applications, please?

I have none.

You have none! Did you keep no copies? Or are you telling me that you didn't apply for any jobs? If you did, I want details, please.

I spoke to someone about one job. But I can't remember the details. It was at a party.

Did I understand you to say earlier that you were competent at your job?

I believe that I was.

And you ask the court to accept that you, a competent accountant, suffered persecution for over eighteen months, were in constant danger of losing your job, with five children to support, but you only applied for one other job, which you heard of at a party and can't remember anything about?

(This last was a rhetorical question. Such questions should not be used too freely, for they elicit no information. But it sometimes has a salutary effect upon a witness to disclose to him clearly the weakness of his position.)

Other lines of inquiry which will be suggested by an imaginative effort to put oneself in the witness's place are illustrated by questions like these:

Did you tell your partner about it?

(This can perhaps be checked against the partner's evidence.)

Where did you get the money?

(Account books or bank statements may later be called for.)

If you really loved her, was it not a florist you should have visited instead of a lawyer?

Why didn't you write a letter?

If he was so drunk, why did you risk your life in his car?

If that's what you felt, why did you continue to deal with him?

When the temperament of the witness is in issue (as it might be, for example, in a matrimonial case), counsel may be able, by circumspect questioning, to get the witness to reveal his tendencies under cross-examination. If, for example, it is the wife's case that her husband is a mean and suspicious man, and that is of importance, counsel cross-examining the husband will, with apparent ingenuousness, engage him in a discussion of the wife's handling of money, her financial needs, her tastes and her habits. Unless the witness is very intelligent, and capable of great self-control, he is likely, while answering questions about such matters, to reveal his mean and suspicious nature if he has one.

Similarly, if counsel believes that the witness is given to ready fabrication, he may find it useful to offer the witness opportunities for improvising, in order to make his tendency plain to the court. Ideally, this will be done in respect of some point on which counsel will be able to refute the fabrication, if it comes. But even when that is not possible, the witness, given the opportunity, will sometimes carry his inventiveness to a point at which it is clear to the court that he is inventing.

A witness to a motor-car accident appears to counsel for the defendant to be untruthful, and willing to say anything which is likely to help the plaintiff. He has already done so by saying that he examined the road surface and saw certain brake marks. Counsel decides to exploit the readiness of the witness to invent:

Do you know whether the plaintiff's car was dripping oil before the collision?

(It was not, and oil leaks have nothing to do with the case.)

CROSS-EXAMINATION

I never examined the car.

When you inspected the southern half of the road did you see any drops of oil on it?

(There would not have been any, and counsel can show it. But the witness thinks that counsel has information that the plaintiff's car was leaking oil, and he says:)

Yes. There were some.

Did they stop short of the point of impact?

No. They led right up to it.

You can't say from what vehicle they came, can you?

Well, I can say this: the line of oil drops ran between the plaintiff's tyre tracks.

For how far back?

For as far back as I inspected the road.

How far apart were the drops?

It's hard to say. Maybe a foot. I may be quite wrong after all this time.

Other people who inspected the road didn't see any oil.

I can't help that. I saw it.

I shall call a mechanic who examined the plaintiff's car carefully, shortly before the impact, and he will say that there was no oil leak.

I take it an oil leak can start at any time.

But what if the same mechanic says that after the impact he again examined the car and it still was not leaking oil?

A similar approach might succeed with a witness of the same type who claims, falsely, to have been at a particular interview:

Do you remember any interruptions of the negotiations?

I can't recollect one at the moment.

If the telephone had rung, would you have remembered that?

Oh, I didn't think you meant interruptions by telephone. Yes, that did happen.

How many times?

That is hard to remember. I can't swear to more than once.

GEORGE COLMAN, Q.C.

Can you tell me whether the plaintiff, in answering the telephone, spoke angrily to the person at the other end?

I can't recollect. If you could remind me it might come back to me.

I do not propose to remind you of any thing. Did you notice any sign of impatience?

I do remember his banging the receiver down rather forcibly. But I hadn't been paying attention to what he said, so it may not have been intentional.

Was there anything to prevent you from hearing what he said?

Not if I'd wanted to. I just took no notice. I was probably looking at my notes while he spoke.

If you were looking at your notes, how did you see him banging the receiver down?

I didn't say I saw it. I heard it. And when I heard it I looked up— his hand was just leaving the phone.

I shall call witnesses—twenty witnesses if necessary—to say that there was no telephone in that room. The phone was in the adjoining room, where you could not have seen it. What do you say now?

A subject upon which counsel will speculate, in relation to a witness whom he believes to be untruthful, is why that witness should lie. Sometimes the motive is obvious, but often it is not. If any theory presents itself, counsel should investigate it. It is to be remembered that it is not only a financial or other interest in the outcome of the suit, or a desire to help one of the litigants, which can induce untruthfulness. The witness may have some personal interest or secret, quite irrelevant to the suit, which he wishes to protect, and which he can protect only by lying. When something of that sort is suspected, counsel will, as a rule, try to expose the motive. But there are cases in which he may feel that, by protecting the witness's personal secret in some way, he can persuade him to be candid about what is relevant to the case. Thus:

CROSS-EXAMINATION

I can understand that if there was a lady with you, you may not wish to disclose her identity. I don't care who she was, and I promise not to ask you. But there was a woman in the car, wasn't there?

Or, in a somewhat different situation:

No one will accuse you of cowardice, Sergeant. It would have been absurd for you to risk your life with things as they were. But you did lock your door, didn't you?

The discussion, up to now, in this chapter, has been of possible ways of obtaining helpful answers from the witness himself, with little or no relation to what other witnesses on the same side have said, or will say. But, very often, counsel's main hope of exposing an untruthful witness will be through conflicts between his testimony and that of others who, on the vital point, support him. It should be stressed that differences between witnesses on matters of detail do not necessarily mean that they, or any of them, are lying. In many cases such differences are to be expected: witnesses may see things from different points of view; a detail which impresses one may not impress others; powers of observation and recollection vary. Much depends, therefore, upon the nature of the divergencies: counsel's efforts will be directed towards eliciting differences which would not be expected in the evidence of truthful witnesses.

He may derive assistance, however, from an inability on the part of an untruthful witness to appreciate this distinction. Such a witness may, when his attention is directed to even the most trifling discrepancy between what he has said and the version of another witness on the same side, seek dishonestly to close the gap, and thereby reveal his own dishonesty.

You said: 'So I put on my coat and left.' Mr. Green, your partner, told the court that you carried your coat out of the building and stopped to put it on in the street.

GEORGE COLMAN, Q.C.

From an honest witness the response would probably be:

> He may be perfectly right. I don't really remember putting on my coat. I just assumed I'd done so. It's an entirely unimportant detail and I shouldn't really have mentioned it at all.

But a perjurer, sensitive about his dishonesty, may try to reconcile the two versions by saying:

> Did I say I put on my coat and then left?
> *That was the effect of your answer. Was it true?*
> I meant to say I started to put on my coat, then decided to take it off again. It was very warm in there. I actually put it on in the street.
> *You remember that clearly?*
> Yes.
> *What on earth makes you remember it?*

But it is the more important discrepancies in which counsel is really interested. In probing for them he will bear in mind that two untruthful witnesses to the same incident will probably have conferred, and agreed upon the details to which they will testify. It is difficult for such witnesses to discuss and remember every detail, but counsel's dilemma is this: they will have prepared themselves on everything that is important, and with regard to what is trivial differences of recollection may not seem significant to the court.

The problem, therefore, is to think of questions which the witnesses are unlikely to have expected, but which, nevertheless, relate to matters which they ought to remember, and about which their recollections should agree, if they are truthful. Here, again, counsel's success or failure is likely to depend upon his powers of imagination. If the fact in issue is, as in a previous example, whether or not the witnesses were present at a meeting, they will probably be ready for a question like this one:

CROSS-EXAMINATION

Did you sit on his left, or he on yours?

or

Did Black sign with his own pen, or was he handed one?

or

Who was it who first mentioned a deposit?

But they may not have been so careful in preparing an account of the manner in which they went to the meeting, and something may come of such approaches as:

Did you walk or take a taxi?
Do you remember meeting anyone on the way?
Where did you meet each other?
Where and how did you arrange to meet?
Did he keep you waiting?
What did you talk about on the way back?
Was either of you carrying anything?
Were you kept waiting? Where did you wait? For how long? Who told you to wait? What did she say?

Witnesses to an alibi often claim that they were gambling together at the time, when, in fact, one of them was elsewhere. Useful questions to put to them, in addition to those which have already been suggested, are:

Did you have anything to eat or drink during the game?—What was it? What did the others drink?—Where did it come from?
Who won?—Who lost? How much did you collect (or pay)?—To or from whom?—Was it paid in notes? Of what denomination were the notes?

GEORGE COLMAN, Q.C.

A very real difficulty faces counsel when the untruthful witnesses have agreed to speak of an occasion when they were in truth together but to graft on to it the detail relevant to the case, or to say that the events of that day took place on another date—the one relevant to the case. Thus, if the man who committed a robbery on the evening of 4th April was in fact playing cards with friends throughout the previous evening, it is easy for his friends to say that the card-game took place on the 4th. They will thus be able to answer, convincingly, all that may be asked about the evening's events. And for searching questions about their reasons for being sure of the date they will be well prepared. They may say, for example, that they read of the robbery in the next morning's newspaper. As far as the writer is aware, there is no effective way of breaking down a false alibi of this kind. If the credibility of the witnesses is to be broken, it will have to be done by cross-examination about matters other than the details of their conduct on the relevant date.

Chapter VI
Risks

A fear which is properly present to the mind of the able cross-examiner is that a line of questioning, or even a single question of his, may destroy or weaken his own case. But, often enough, risks should be taken. There is a traditional dictum, but a fallacious one, that cross-examining counsel should never put a question unless he knows that the answer will be favourable to his own case. No one who follows such a precept can discharge his function as a cross-examiner properly. Nor is the rule a sound one in either of these modified forms: 'Never put a question unless you have *good reason to believe* that the answer will be favourable to you', or 'Never put an *important* question if the answer may be unfavourable'.

Unfortunately, cross-examination is too complicated and subtle a process to be patient of such dogmatic instruction. The most that can be said is that questions should be so chosen, and so framed, that unjustifiable risks are avoided. And the question whether a risk is justifiable or not can be judged only in the light of the complex of facts and probabilities which are, or should be, in the mind of counsel at the time when his decision comes to be made.

An example of a wholly unjustified risk is to be found in the situation where the answer to a question cannot materially strengthen the cross-examiner's case, and may seriously weaken it: A plaintiff is relying upon a material false representation as a ground for avoiding a contract with the defendant. He testifies that the misrepresentation was made in a telegram, and he proves its falsity. But the

GEORGE COLMAN, Q.C.

telegram was sent, on a Friday at noon, to his country home; and his evidence discloses that he spent the whole of that Friday in a city two hundred miles away from his country home, and signed the contract there at four o'clock on the Friday afternoon.

There is nothing in the evidence in chief to suggest that, in these circumstances, the misrepresentation in the telegram could have played any part in inducing the plaintiff to contract, and counsel for the defendant will have noticed this vital hiatus in the plaintiff's testimony. Such things should not happen in lawsuits, but they do. The reason may be ineptitude on the part of the plaintiff's counsel, or it may be that his client has made a statement in his evidence which counsel could not have foreseen, and was unable to correct.

Cross-examining counsel may be tempted to put this question:

So the telegram had nothing to do with your decision to sign the contract?

The temptation may be induced by more than the desire of an orderly mind to round things off logically. There is great personal satisfaction in bringing off a dramatic coup: and it impresses one's client and one's audience, whereas silence, or an undramatic and possibly unfruitful cross-examination on other aspects of the case, will not. But counsel's function is not to provide drama, or to build up a reputation for himself as a deadly cross-examiner. His point can be effectively, if less spectacularly, made after the plaintiff's case has been closed. And if he is so unwise as to put his question, what may follow is something like this:

It had a good deal to do with my decision.
But you didn't see the telegram until after you had signed?
That is true. But I phoned to the country at about three o'clock and my wife read it to me. Because of what was in it, I decided to do the deal.

This may not be true; it may be the extempore invention of an unscrupulous witness. But it may be impossible to disprove what he said, and the defendant may lose his case as a direct result of the ill-judged question.

Thus starkly presented, the unwisdom of asking the question is obvious. But here, again, the example has been over-simplified for the sake of brevity and clarity. In practice, parallel cases will arise when the facts are not so clear-cut, and where the logic of the situation tends to be obscured by the other issues.

There are cases in which it is necessary to run the risk of a damaging answer. One such case is where counsel is under an obligation to put to a witness what his own witnesses will say: he must discharge that duty, no matter what the response is likely to be. But there are other cases, and the clearest of those is the one where the suit will, in any event, be lost if the risk is not taken. Similarly, where the testimony of a witness is likely to be accepted unless it is weakened or destroyed by cross-examination, it may be wise, if no better line of attack is open, to put questions at the risk that the answer may strengthen the evidence already given.

A witness testifies that at 3 a.m., soon after a house had been broken into and some clothing stolen therefrom, he saw the accused hurrying away from the house carrying a number of suits and dresses. As he approached, the witness says, the accused broke into a run and disappeared round a corner. Counsel for the accused has been instructed that his client was nowhere near the burgled house at the time. The soundness of the identification is thus vital.

Counsel tests the witness's veracity and reliability by asking him to explain his presence near the house at 3 a.m., by calling for details of the surroundings, by inquiring into the subsequent conduct of the witness, and in other ways. The answers are convincing. Questions about the clothing and build of the man said to have been the accused yield nothing to cast doubt on the identification. But evidence about the sources of light, times and positions may then justify these questions:

So you were, at your closest, twenty yards away from him?
Yes.

And you saw his face only during the three or four seconds before he turned to his right and ran?

Yes.

And during those three or four seconds you weren't suspicious?

Well, I thought it unusual—I don't know what you mean by suspicious.

You didn't think you were looking at a burglar and would have to give evidence about it some day?

I won't say I had that thought; but I was interested in him.

Why?

Because of the clothes, and the time of night, and because he was hurrying.

But you didn't think it necessary to study his features?

I didn't think about his features. But I saw them and it was the accused.

You think it was the accused. But you can make mistakes, can't you?

I can make mistakes. But I'm not making one now.

Do you suggest that the light was good?

No, but it was good enough for me to see his face.

The witness appears to be unbiased and candid. His evidence will carry great weight against the denial of the accused. It is therefore important, if possible, to establish a reasonable possibility that he is mistaken in his identification. Counsel must decide whether he should risk asking a question like this one:

This face, which you saw for a few seconds, in poor light, was a face which you'd never seen in your life before, wasn't it?

An affirmative answer will form the basis for an argument that there is room for honest error on the part of the witness. But the argument will be a very weak one indeed if the witness responds by saying:

Oh, no. He doesn't know me, but I've seen him hundreds of times. He used to travel every day on the same bus as I did.

CROSS-EXAMINATION

Despite the danger of some such answer, it would probably be advisable to put the question. It is more likely than not that the answer will be a favourable one. And without it the evidence of identification will almost certainly carry great weight. Moreover, an apparently unfavourable answer may turn out to be a starting point for a further series of questions in response to which the witness may reveal himself as less reliable than he has thus far appeared. It may well be possible, by asking questions about the bus journeys, to whittle the 'hundreds of times' down to a dozen occasions or so. This witness's recollection of the dates and times may prove demonstrably incorrect. Or it may be possible, on the basis of what is extracted from him, to argue cogently that he saw a man who looked something like the man he had often seen on the bus, and that the confidence with which he puts forward his identification flows from the unconscious elevation of that similarity into an identity.

The decision whether to risk an unfavourable answer or not must thus depend largely upon counsel's assessment of the danger that such an answer will be given, the consequences to his case if it is given, and the equally important consequences which can be expected if he leaves his question unasked.

Another important factor is counsel's assessment of his witness. He may judge the witness to be one who is unlikely to give the unfavourable response which he fears. Or, on the other hand, he may take the opposite view. If, for example, he judges the witness to be unscrupulous and crafty, he will be aware of the danger that, if an opening is given, the witness will seize upon it, and give a damaging answer, even if it is untrue.

If, of course, the adverse answer is likely to be demonstrably untrue, it may be welcomed. This, indeed, is a situation in which the skilled cross-examiner may deliberately invite an adverse answer, basing himself, again, upon his judgment of the witness and the prospect that the answer, if it is unfavourable, will be one which he can show to be untrue. If he can do that, he will thereby destroy or weaken the effect of the other evidence which the witness has given.

GEORGE COLMAN, Q.C.

Such an occasion might arise in a matrimonial dispute. A bitter wife is testifying about the behaviour of her spouse. As her evidence goes on she gains confidence and her complaints multiply and are expressed with growing vehemence. Her husband was selfish, he was neglectful, he was mean, he was surly, he was insulting in private, he was insulting in public, he made outrageous and unfounded accusations against her, even in the presence of their children. Cross-examining counsel suspects that much of the testimony is exaggerated, if not false. He has before him the pleadings, as well as a long letter written on behalf of the wife by her solicitor shortly before the institution of the action. Her complaints are set out in these documents, but not in the detail or with the vehemence that characterizes the wife's evidence. He decides to encourage her to be untruthful, if that, indeed, is her tendency—

He used to say that you were extravagant?
Yes.
And that was untrue?
Yes.
He said you were lazy, although he knew you were not?
Yes.
He called you a fool and a half-wit?
Yes.
Are those the gross insults you complained of in your letter?
Some of them.
Are you suggesting there was anything worse?
Yes, I am.
What was worse? He didn't call you a thief, did he?
No, but he called me other things.
What other things?
All sorts of things.
You say that there were worse insults than the ones which I have mentioned. What were they?
He said that I was a whore.
He used that word?

CROSS-EXAMINATION

Yes, he did.

Often?

Yes, often.

Not in front of your children, I trust?

Yes, in front of my children.

Regularly?

No, once only.

Do you remember it well?

I'll never forget it. It's the most humiliating thing that ever happened to me.

What did you do when he said that?

I just walked out of the room.

You made no protest?

I was afraid to. He was violent.

Do you mean that you thought he might hit you?

Yes.

Did you have the slightest basis for that fear?

Yes, I did.

Just your womanly instinct?

No, he said he'd hit me.

Did you believe him?

Yes, he'd hit me once before, in the face.

When?

A few weeks before—not very hard.

Counsel has achieved his object. He continues:

So he hit you in the face on one occasion, then threatened to hit you again, and called you a whore in front of your children?

Yes.

These things hurt you deeply?

The smack didn't hurt much.

These things humiliated you deeply?

Yes.

Why were they not mentioned in your evidence in chief?

GEORGE COLMAN, Q.C.

I wasn't asked about them.

Why were they not mentioned in your pleadings?

I don't know about pleadings. I didn't draw them up.

Why were they not referred to in your solicitor's letter?

I told him about them. But I told him so many things. He must have overlooked these.

He remembered to complain that your husband said you were lazy, but not that he called you a whore in front of your children?

It must be so.

And he forgot that your husband had struck you?

I suppose so—or perhaps I forgot to tell him.

But you said you did tell him?

I think I did—I'm not sure.

So you think that you may have forgotten to tell him?

Here the apparently damaging answers which counsel invited have proved fatal to the credibility of the witness. And he was taking no real risk.

When counsel is inclined to take the risk of a truly damaging answer, he can decrease the risk by feeling his way carefully towards the critical question. Again a matrimonial suit will furnish an example.

It is averred against the wife that she committed adultery, and also that she habitually neglected and ill-treated her young children. She will, in due course, deny both allegations. A woman who lived in the flat next door is called to speak of an occasion when she saw a strange man leaving the wife's flat late at night when her husband was away. She says nothing about the children in her evidence in chief. Cross-examining counsel, having done what he could on the adultery issue, is tempted to seek, from this witness, favourable evidence about his client's treatment of her children. But instead of tackling the question bluntly, he works carefully towards it:

Did you go rushing to tell the plaintiff what you had seen?

I did not.

CROSS-EXAMINATION

Were you not keen to give evidence against my client?
No.
Would it be fair to say that you dislike her?
I neither like her nor dislike her.

Thus far, counsel has been hinting at bias and relying on the general rule (discussed elsewhere in this book) that witnesses are sensitive to suggestions of bias and often willing to go out of their way to disprove it. He continues:

So you have nothing against her?
No.
She had done nothing to annoy you or irritate you?
No.
Apart from the incident of which you have spoken she has done nothing to make you disapprove of her?
Nothing that I know of.
You were close neighbours for two years and you saw her several times a day?
Yes, but we hardly spoke to each other.
Was that because you disapproved of her or disliked her?
I've told you, I didn't.
Perhaps her children got on your nerves?

The witness, still resenting an imputation of bias, may here tend to exaggerate her true feelings.

Not at all. They were delightful children.
Would you say pleasant, attractive, clean, cheerful youngsters?
Yes, I would.
That was the impression they made on you whenever you saw them?
Yes.
Do you mean when they were with their mother, or also when they were alone?
Always.

In fact, until the night of which you have spoken my client's family seemed to you to be an ordinary decent, normal family?
Yes.

Counsel has achieved his object, and he was not taking an undue risk; if the witness had been able to speak of any substantial neglect or ill-treatment of the children she would probably have done so in her evidence in chief. But there was some risk that (particularly if she was biased against the wife) she would have taken the opportunity to say something derogatory during the cross-examination. The method adopted has reduced the risk of that; if counsel had sensed, at any stage, that he was not going to achieve his object, he could have discontinued his line of questioning. He might even have been presented with an opening for an altered approach, designed to show that the witness was, indeed, biased.

In the following example counsel has adopted a similar approach to the witness. But he has tried to make use of her vanity.

It is alleged that the accused was a participant in a fraud on a bank. She was a typist in the bank and counsel hopes to be able to show, through witnesses yet to be called, that she could have played a part in the fraud only if, on frequent occasions during banking hours, she left her desk in the typing-room and went to the ledger department of the bank. Prosecuting counsel has called, on another point, a female bank official who was in control of the typing-room, and defending counsel would like, if possible, to establish, through her, an improbability that the accused often went to the ledger department. But he senses danger. The witness is a somewhat overbearing spinster. Counsel judges her to be an arrogant and self-important person with little liking or sympathy for the accused, or indeed for any of the young typists in the bank. He edges his way towards the critical question:

How long have you worked for the bank?
Over thirty years; do you want the exact dates?
No. That's near enough. I take it that you had acquired a thorough knowledge of the bank's routine?

Well, what do you think I was doing those thirty years? I'm not a fool.

I'm sure you are not. Would it be fair to say that you are an able, loyal, trusted servant of the bank?

I call myself an official, not a servant. I am loyal and I'm sure they trust me. As to my ability—well, why did they put me in charge of the typing-room?

Is that a difficult job?

I don't find it difficult. But it's not a simple matter to supervise and control twenty young girls—especially the type you get these days.

They have to be closely watched, do they?

They do. Some of them will take advantage the moment you turn your back. And the mistakes!

So you have to be stern with them?

Well—firm.

If you find one of the girls doing anything irregular, you deal with it; you reprimand her or report her?

I do.

Am I right in thinking that you have to watch them all closely, and deal with any irregularity promptly and firmly?

You are quite right.

The accused had no business in the ledger department?

Not unless I sent her there. I think I did on one occasion.

But she had no right to go wandering off from her desk into the ledger department whenever she pleased?

Certainly not.

That would have been an irregularity which you would have dealt with, promptly and firmly?

Yes. But I think I see what you are getting at, and I want to say this: I have no eyes in the back of my head; I don't say it's impossible for a girl to slip out of the typing-room for a few moments without my noticing it.

But if you did notice it, you'd deal with it?

Certainly.

GEORGE COLMAN, Q.C.

And if a girl did it regularly, you'd be bound to notice it?
Well, it depends how regularly.
You have told me what your duties are. You have told me that one of them is to watch the girls closely. And I understood you to say that you carried out that duty diligently. Am I wrong?
No, I won't say that you are wrong.
So if the accused left her desk and went into the ledger department several times a week, you would have noticed it, and dealt with it?
Several times a week. ... Yes.
But you didn't notice or deal with anything like that?
You mean with the accused?
Yes. The accused going to the ledger department?
No, I didn't notice that.
Then we can safely take it that it didn't happen?
Yes.

The risk was taken, and the desired result was achieved. It might have been achieved if counsel had come boldly and immediately to the point; but, human quirks being what they are, it might not.

There are other occasions when it is wiser not to take the risk of an unfavourable answer. An obvious case of that sort is this:

A plaintiff has been injured in a collision with a railway train at a level crossing. An independent witness, who happens to have been near by, says that he heard a whistle from the engine of the train several seconds before the collision, although the plaintiff has already testified that he heard no whistle. Counsel for the plaintiff will probably cross-examine about the time and duration of the whistle, the relative positions of the witness, the plaintiff, and the train, the direction of the wind, and matters of that kind. But unless something most unusual in the evidence of the witness justifies it, it would be unwise for him to put a question like this:

I suggest to you that you have been thinking a good deal about the accident and have persuaded yourself that you heard a whistle?

CROSS-EXAMINATION

It has been pointed out in an earlier chapter how rarely a witness can be expected to respond favourably to a question of that kind. The danger is that he will say something like this:

> I have nothing against the plaintiff. I'm sorry for him, and I'd like to see him compensated. So I haven't stretched my imagination against him. But in view of your suggestion I'll tell you that I did not imagine the whistle. I heard it, and I remarked on it to my passenger before the train hit the plaintiff.

(Whether the last part of the answer is admissible as a response to an imputation of recent fabrication is a question which falls outside the scope of this book. But the answer was a damaging one, and it was predictable that it would be.)

The temptation to take a risk is particularly great when counsel, having had a measure of success with a series of questions, would like to put the matter beyond doubt. But this desire may lead him to put a question which will destroy or weaken his previous achievement. The decision must be taken on an assessment of the probable sufficiency, for the purposes of the case, of the success already achieved, weighed against the likelihood that a further answer will be favourable, rather than unfavourable. If counsel is satisfied that what he has achieved will discharge the onus resting on him, or preclude the discharge by his opponent of his onus, the point should be left where it is. If, on the other hand, the measure of success achieved is clearly inadequate for the purposes of the case, it may be necessary to take a risk. But when (as so often happens) neither of these situations can be said clearly to exist, a decision has to be taken on counsel's assessment of the witness.

In the cross-examination of the bank official which appears earlier in this chapter it was safe to ask the final question, because the answer could hardly have been unfavourable. If the witness had, for some reason, chosen to give a negative answer, or an equivocal one, counsel, on the basis of what she had already said, would almost certainly have been able by further questioning, to drive her to a favourable reponse.

But with some witnesses, and in some situations, the desire to deliver a *coup de grâce* would be better resisted. In an accident case, counsel for the defendant has had a measure of success in cross-examining a candid medical expert on the question whether the plaintiff's injury will produce traumatic arthritis in later years. He has reached this stage:

> *So it will depend on a number of factors whether there will be arthritis or not?*
> Yes.
> *And many of these factors are unpredictable?*
> Some of them certainly are.
> *What is more, the X-ray plates are not clear enough to give you all the information you would have liked to have before making a prognosis?*
> No. That is one of my difficulties.
> *You cannot be certain that arthritis will ever appear?*
> No.
> *Or when it will appear if it does develop?*
> No.

That is substantial success. And (unless the point has already been made, adversely to his client) counsel might be acting unwisely if he seeks to round off his line of inquiry by putting this question:

> *In fact it is improbable that there will be arthritis?*

For the answer, unless there was a firm foundation for optimism, may well be:

> No. I can't say that. There are all these uncertainties, but even if I allow fully for them, I must say that I think it probable that he'll have arthritis within ten years.

CROSS-EXAMINATION

In assessing the risk that a particular question will elicit an unfavourable answer, counsel will be assisted, very often, by his preparation of the case, and by his knowledge of the habits and temperament of opposing counsel. It is often safe to assume that if the witness were able and willing to give the adverse answer, it would have been mentioned by him in some document, or reflected in the pleadings, or drawn from him during his examination in chief. But the two *indiciae* last mentioned may be misleading if the draftsman of the pleadings, or counsel who led the evidence in chief, was a careless person, or had inadequate opportunities for finding out all that the witness could say.

When counsel decides that he must or should take the risk of asking a question which may produce a damaging answer, he will, if possible, first take steps to reduce the extent of the risk. How that can sometimes be done will appear from the examples in other chapters.

Chapter VII
Honest Witnesses

A reader may, understandably, react to this chapter heading by pointing out that, as often as not, a cross-examiner does not know, when he starts to cross-examine a witness, whether that witness is honest or dishonest; and often he remains in doubt about that throughout. That is true; and it is one of the reasons why the discussion of multiple aims in cross-examination which appears in the first chapter of this book remains relevant here, as elsewhere. What follows has a bearing upon the witness (and there are many such) who is known or believed by counsel to be honest, in the sense that he is telling the truth as he sees it. It has a bearing also upon witnesses who may or may not be truthful; with them counsel will combine the approaches here described with others mentioned elsewhere in this book. And, because it is not possible to keep a discussion of the techniques of cross-examination within closed compartments, much of what appears on the immediately succeeding pages is appropriate for use, on occasions, with witnesses who are not honest at all.

If a witness is known to be honest, or if he appears to be so, and there is no substantial prospect of showing that he is not, the wise cross-examiner will sometimes elect to put no questions at all. But that is not always the appropriate course to take, because honest witnesses can be mistaken; or there may be useful evidence which they can give in addition to what they have already said. And because of their honesty the correction of their errors, and the amplification

CROSS-EXAMINATION

of their testimony, will be more easily achieved than it would be if they were astute to deceive or to suppress.

A clergyman has deposed to some slanderous words spoken by the defendant about the plaintiff at a church meeting. He has given his evidence fairly and intelligently, and there is no prospect of showing that his account of what took place is in any respect inaccurate. But it does not follow that he should not be cross-examined. If the defence, or one of the defences, is that the words were spoken on a privileged occasion, the clergyman may be an admirable witness through whom the relevant facts can be established. Or counsel may be able, by putting appropriate questions to the clergyman, to elicit evidence which will operate in reduction of damages:

Were you distressed to hear these things said about a member of your congregation?
Grievously so, sir, grievously.
You believed that it was an unjustified attack?
I did, and I still do.
As far as you could judge, was the plaintiff as distressed as you were?
It's not an easy thing to look into a woman's heart. All I can say is that she took it well—very well.
Will you agree that she simply shrugged her shoulders and smiled?
Yes. I noticed that.
I suppose you spoke to her after the meeting, did you?
I felt it my Christian duty to seek her out and offer my sympathy.
What did she say about the incident?
Forgive my raising it; but am I allowed to tell what other people have said to me?
If it was told to you in confidence I may not press you. But if not, you are allowed to answer my question, and I ask you to do so.
She said: 'Don't worry about my feelings, I take it from whence it comes!'
What did that convey to you?
That she wasn't very much concerned with the attack because of the sort of person the defendant was.

What sort of person was the defendant?

Really, I'd rather not express an opinion, unless I must.

Can we say a little imaginative and irresponsible? Is that how you assessed her?

She was that.

And she was known to be that by everyone there?

That was the general feeling, I should think.

Can I take it that you didn't believe the accusation, and no one else did either?

You must not ask me to speak positively on oath about the views of other people. But I told them all what I thought, and I have no reason to think that anyone disagreed with me.

Did you, perhaps, tell them not to repeat the slander?

Indeed I did. It was for that very purpose that I got them all together after the meeting was over.

Are they responsible people?

I think so.

Would It be right, then, to say this: that the incident did not diminish your respect or regard for the plaintiff, or, probably, the regard or respect for her which any of the others present had?

I think that's fair enough.

And it is unlikely that, until this case began, anyone else knew what had been said?

I suppose the plaintiff told her husband. Apart from that, and apart from the lawyers, I would agree with what you say.

Similarly, it may be possible, without disputing the facts to which a truthful witness has deposed, to elicit from him further information which puts those facts in a different light. An example may be taken from a murder case in which a witness has said that on the day of the murder, he saw the accused wrapping up a revolver in brown paper and hiding it behind some books on the top shelf of a tall bookcase:

Did you see what he was doing with the revolver before he wrapped it up?

CROSS-EXAMINATION

No. He was doing something to it with a cloth.

He will say that he was oiling it. Can you dispute that?

No.

Whatever he was doing, he was doing in front of a large ground floor window, was he not?

Yes. That's the window through which I saw him.

The lights were on in the room. And the curtains were wide open; do you agree?

Yes.

And dozens of people pass that window at that time of the evening, don't they?

Many people do.

And although everybody in the neighbourhood must by then have heard of the murder, the accused was displaying the revolver quite openly, was he not?

At that stage, yes.

Now I shall come to the later stage. When you say he hid the revolver, all you mean, I take it, was that he put it behind the books?

Well, that and wrapping it in brown paper.

But he wrapped it up and put it behind the books, still with his curtain open, so that any passer-by could see. Is that not so?

Yes.

If you had an oily object which you wanted to put away among your other belongings, what would you do with it?

Wrap it up, I suppose.

Of course. Now tell me this: was there not a rumour that day that the shot had been fired by a child from his father's rifle?

I didn't hear that.

The accused will say that he heard it, and that it reminded him of his revolver. He has three young children in his house, hasn't he?

Yes, he has.

You know the house. Can you suggest any better place in which to put the revolver out of sight and out of reach of the children?

A locked drawer or a locked cupboard, perhaps.

Have you ever seen the wife of the accused looking for her bunch of keys?

She's always looking for her bunch of keys.

What do you say now about the place where the accused put the revolver?

I'm with you. Perhaps it was the best place if he wanted to keep it away from the children.

There are situations in which a witness, if supplied with information not previously available to him, will modify or retract an answer which he has previously given. Thus:

You have said, as an experienced grocer, that he could never have hoped to make a living in that shop, paying the rent which was mentioned to you?

Yes. It's a poor neighbourhood. And there's a more attractive grocery shop a few doors away.

But what if he had been promised that the hospital would buy all its groceries from him?

Oh, that's quite different. He could have made a living from the hospital contract alone.

Or, in a stabbing case:

You say that this was the knife which was used?

I'm pretty certain of it. Either that knife or a very similar one.

Take the knife, and this scale. How long is the blade?

I make it two and a half inches.

So do I. Now what do you say if I tell you that at the post-mortem the fatal wound was found to be four inches deep?

If that is so, I must have been completely mistaken. It couldn't have been this knife.

Or one like it?

Not one of similar size.

However sincere a witness may be, the reliability of his evidence depends, in large measure, upon his opportunities for accurate observation. It is therefore important, sometimes, to investigate

CROSS-EXAMINATION

carefully the physical position which the witness occupied, the lighting conditions, the time available for his observations, his state of mind during that period, and the extent to which his vision may have been obstructed or his attention divided. This is true, particularly, of witnesses to complicated or fast-moving events, like motor accidents and fights.

One of the great difficulties which faces a court hearing the testimony of eyewitnesses, is the tendency of human beings, even the most honest of them, to fill by inference or imagination the gaps in their observation. Usually they are quite unconscious of having done so, and come to believe that they really saw what in fact they assumed. The process of mental reconstruction tends to begin almost at once. And by the time the witness has been thinking and talking about his experience for a few days, he believes firmly that he saw more than in fact he did. For that reason it is seldom possible, by means of cross-examination, to obtain, even from a candid witness, an admission that part of his testimony is based on inference, not observation. But what counsel can do is to elicit evidence of the circumstances from which the court will infer that some of the evidence relates to details which the witness could not have observed, or probably did not observe, although he is convinced that he did. Sometimes it is possible to show what the mental process was. That usually happens with a very simple witness, as in the following example:

After the quarrel about the liquor, you say, the accused and his two friends stood up?
Yes.
What weapons did you see at that stage?
Only the knife, which the man in the red jersey had. He drew the knife, and then the accused shot me in the leg.
The accused will deny that he shot you, and he will say that he had no firearm. Others will support him on that. Where did the firearm come from?
I didn't see.

GEORGE COLMAN, Q.C.

What did it look like?

I didn't see it. Someone put the lights out just before the shot was
fired.

*But if someone put the lights out, how do you know that it was the accused
who shot you?*

I knew he owned a revolver; and I'd always felt that he hated me.

Similarly, it is sometimes possible to expose as hearsay what, on
the face of it, is direct observation by the witness.

*Mr. Brown will say that in your discussion of the contract there was no
mention of the cancellation clause. Do you dispute that?*

Perhaps there wasn't. But before he signed the contract he read
it through carefully.

Didn't he sign the contract that very afternoon, in your office?

Yes.

*There are about twenty typed pages of it. Did you sit and watch him read-
ing it?*

No. During our discussion I was called to the next office. I told
Mr. Brown I'd be away about five minutes; in fact I was away for
about half an hour.

And what was he doing when you got back?

Looking out of the window.

What happened then?

He said he had a plane to catch, and we'd better sign at once.
So we did.

How do you know that he read the contract carefully?

My late wife told me. She came to see me (you know how women
will just burst into an office) and she said that he was poring
over a document.

Personal vanity may cause an otherwise truthful witness to give
misleading testimony. The cross-examiner will, if he sees or suspects that, take one of two courses. He may seek to cushion the
blow to self-esteem, and thereby persuade the witness to correct

CROSS-EXAMINATION

or moderate his evidence. Or, if he feels that such an approach is unlikely to succeed, he may ask questions designed to reveal to the court the vanity which is, or may be, colouring the evidence of the witness. Thus, to a cashier:

> *You say that you made no mistake about the amount?*
> No.
> *I am going to suggest that you possibly did. Please bear with me before you comment. It was nearly closing time, wasn't it?* Yes, but. . . .
> *Please! You were terribly rushed, I understand?*
> Yes.
> *Have you any idea how many transactions you'd handled that day?*
> About five hundred, I'd guess.
> *On my rough calculations, based on the books, it was about seven hundred. In seven hours work that's about one hundred an hour isn't it?*
> It was eight hours. I worked through my lunch hour that day.
> *I've made another rough calculation. You handled about three thousand transactions a week. Is that about right?*
> At least that.
> *So in your five years with the firm you had handled about* 750,000 *cash transactions?*
> Yes, and I've never been shown to have made a mistake.
> *That's just my point. We all make mistakes sometimes: all of us, I assure you. Is it so impossible that you, at the end of a long, hard day, could have made one single slip—one slip in* 750,000 *transactions?*
> Well, I suppose it is possible.

If the answer is negative, counsel will be driven to the alternative approach:

> *Do you never make mistakes about anything at all?*
> Not many, and none with figures.
> *Do you claim to be unusually gifted?*
> I've been told that I have an outstanding capacity for figures.
> *Have you never made a mistake with figures?*

GEORGE COLMAN, Q.C.

It may seem strange to you, but I'm really incapable of such a mistake. Figures come to me like breathing to you.

Do I take it that when you've added up a column of figures you don't check your calculation?

It's quite unnecessary.

And you didn't do it on this occasion?

No. I tell you it wasn't necessary. The figure was correct.

Tell me, have you never in your life made a mistake with figures?

Honestly, I can't remember one.

Not even when you were at school?

I always got 100 per cent for arithmetic.

Don't you think that you ought to be something more important than the cashier in a department store?

Frankly, I think I should be; and I have no doubt that I soon will be.

Another personal weakness which sometimes requires to be revealed by counsel in order that the evidence of a witness may be properly evaluated is bias. The witness is often quite unconscious of his bias, or at any rate, of the manner in which it has coloured his observation, recollection, and testimony. And it is, therefore, seldom possible to obtain from him an admission that anything of that sort has happened. But even that is possible with an exceptionally candid witness like the headmistress of a girls' school in the following example:

I suppose you hate the idea that a girl from your school could behave like a prostitute. Do you?

I hate the idea of anyone behaving in that way.

But particularly a girl from your school, surely?

Of course. And one of the reasons is that it's likely to be a false idea if it's applied to one of those girls.

They have the same human weaknesses as other people, haven't they?

Weaknesses can be controlled. And if my life's work means anything at all, my girls are in control of themselves.

CROSS-EXAMINATION

You really believe that?

I really believe that.

So you are inclined to give Jane the benefit of the doubt?

Isn't that what the law requires?

I was asking you about your own state of mind. You are hoping that these suggestions will be proved untrue?

Fervently; and I believe that they will.

That hope, and that belief, you had even when you saw her through the field-glasses?

Yes, I think so.

And at the later stage when you say that she was obviously surprised and distressed?

Yes.

She might have been acting a part, might she not?

I didn't think so.

You didn't want to think so, did you?

No, I suppose I didn't.

That state of mind may have clouded your judgment, don't you think?

Not consciously.

Perhaps unconsciously?

Perhaps.

More frequently, the witness will firmly deny that any conscious or unconscious bias can have influenced his or her testimony. Yet it is well to remember, and to demonstrate, if possible, the fact that children, in their mother's eyes, do not appear as they do to strangers; that the author of a play may hear loud applause when to others the response of the audience seems lukewarm; that an inventor is often blind to the demerits of his invention; that a scientist investigating a favourite theory may tend, unconsciously, to overlook or minimize conflicting data.

Some witnesses are biased against particular classes or groups of people. Often these are dishonest witnesses. But sometimes they are giving their evidence honestly, without the insight which would warn them that their prejudices may have influenced their interpretation or recollection of events. That is why they are discussed in this chapter. Counsel should be alert for signs of such bias if it may have affected the attitude of the witness towards someone mentioned in his evidence. Pointers to such prejudice are such things as these: a note of contempt or bitterness in the voice of the witness when speaking of the relevant group or type of persons; a tendency to avoid using a person's name when it would be natural to do so; a tendency to mispronounce the name, or be uncertain about it when that is not to be expected; the use of generalizations (the word 'they' is often significant).

When one of these signs appears, counsel will ask questions designed to reveal the prejudice, if it exists.

> *Were you expecting him to apologize?*
> No. They are not given to making apologies.
> *What do you mean by 'they'?*
> Youths of that type.
> *What type?*
> I mean these people with long hair and blue jeans. You know the sort.
> *You find them ill-mannered, do you?*
> I do.
> *All of them?*
> All I've ever met.
> *And what do you think about their honesty?*
> Seeing you ask me, I wouldn't trust one of them.
> *I take it, then, that the moment you set eyes on the accused in this case you assumed that he was an ill-mannered, dishonest lout?*
> Yes, and what he did next confirmed it.

To take another example:

> *Who was his previous employer?*
> Oh, a Mr. Bloom or something.
> *Are you not sure of the name?*
> It was Bloom.

CROSS-EXAMINATION

I take it you didn't ask Mr. Bloom about him?
I did not.
Why?
I didn't think I'd get the truth.
Tell the court why, please?
Well, you know, they hang together.
Who?
Jews.

In cross-examining some witnesses, counsel may be able to achieve his purpose merely by bringing to their notice facts of which they are not aware. Thus, if a medical man who was a witness to a will has said that the testatrix appeared to him to be of sound mind at the time, this may follow:

How did you come to witness the will?
I was playing chess with the testatrix's employer when her brother asked me if I'd witness her will.
So she was not your patient?
No. I'd never seen her in my life.
You did not know, I take it, that on the previous two nights she had chosen to sleep under her bed instead of on it?
Indeed, no.
What would you have done if you had known that?
I'd certainly have hesitated to witness the will.
What if you had been told that she had telephoned an estate agent at eleven o'clock at night and told him to sell her property in Scotland?
That depends on circumstances.
And if she had no property in Scotland?
I would not have witnessed the will.
If those were the facts, was she of sound mind and understanding?
I doubt it very much.

It is sometimes possible, when cross-examining an honest witness, to extract from him, by the simple application of logic, the concessions which the cross-examiner requires for the purposes of

GEORGE COLMAN, Q.C.

his case. No more may be required of counsel, in such a situation, than an appreciation of the relevant logical steps, and an ability to frame his questions with such clarity that he will be able to carry the candid witness with him, from step to step. The preliminary analysis may be involved, and the clear formulation of the questions may be difficult; but the process will, it is hoped, be sufficiently illustrated by the two very simple examples which follow:

The seller of a business which deals in household crockery has had a restrictive covenant imposed upon him by the purchaser; such a covenant will be enforceable only if it went no further than was reasonably necessary for the protection of the goodwill of the business which was sold, and the purchaser (an honest man) is cross-examined on the question whether the terms of the restraint conformed with that requirement:

> *Let me read you the terms of the restraint, Mr. Green: 'The seller shall not, within a period of three years from the date upon which this sale comes into operation, carry on, within a distance of ten miles from the premises in which he is presently trading (or of any branch of the business which the purchaser may see fit to establish) any business which deals in goods made of china, porcelain or plastic materials.' Did you consider that to be reasonably necessary for the protection of the goodwill which you acquired?*

I did.

> *Would you say it went no further than was reasonably necessary for the proper protection of that goodwill?*

I would. When I drafted it I was trying to be fair to both of us, and I don't think I was unreasonable.

> *The business dealt solely in household crockery, did it not?*

That's what we call it, but I'm not sure of the exact scope of the term crockery. It's plates, cups and saucers, teapots, jugs and so forth. But there are also things like ash-trays, flower vases and soap-dishes; and we took over a big stock of china ornaments. Are all these things crockery?

> *Well, shall we say household utensils and ornaments of all kinds?*

CROSS-EXAMINATION

I think that's fair. Perhaps it's too fair. The business has never dealt in metal utensils like buckets or enamelled basins. The stock is confined to things made of china, porcelain and plastics.

And was the trade in these articles entirely with customers who lived in the neighbourhood?

Mainly, but not entirely. Our town is the centre of quite a large farming area, and the shop is near the station. So we get farmers and their wives dropping in to buy a few things when they come in to town. I think there was quite a bit of that in my predecessor's time, too.

But there was no mail order business, was there?

Not that I know of.

Can I take it, then, that the business had no goodwill among people living, say, a hundred miles away or more?

I don't ask every woman who comes into the shop to buy a teapot where she lives. And nor did your client, I'm sure. There may have been an occasional customer who was visiting our part of the country but who lived in Glasgow or Portsmouth or Hong Kong, or anywhere else.

I understand. But my question was whether or not the business had any goodwill among people who lived far away. To be reasonable, what do you say to that?

Well, to be reasonable, I'd say not.

Now look at the part of the restraint which is in brackets. It refers to any branch of the business which you may see fit to establish.

That is because I thought of opening a branch near the Town Hall if things went well.

No doubt. But there was nothing in the contract, or elsewhere, to prevent you from establishing a branch in Glasgow or Portsmouth, was there?

I suppose not.

And if you did, you would build up a local goodwill there, would you not?

I hope so.

But the goodwill which you bought, as one of the assets of the business, would have nothing to do with the new branch, would it?

115

Not in Glasgow or Portsmouth, no.

Was it, then reasonable to restrain the defendant from competing with you there?

I'd rather not have him competing with me there or anywhere else.

Let me reframe my question. Can you say that it was reasonably necessary for the protection of the goodwill which you bought from the defendant that he be restrained from competing with you in Glasgow?

No.

Or anywhere else a hundred miles or more from the place where he was trading?

No.

Whether you chose to open a branch there or not?

I understand your point. You are right. I went too far.

Now what about the ten-mile radius. How did you get to that?

That's quite a different matter. As I told you, there was trade from the surrounding farms. I thought a ten-mile circle was very fair indeed.

Did you have a map in front of you when you fixed it?

No. I just took a reasonable distance.

Look at this map. I've drawn on it the ten-mile circle referred to in the clause. ... Do you see that the villages of Brownville and Brownton fall just inside it?

Yes. But they never entered by mind.

They are across the river, aren't they, and on a different railway system?

Yes.

Will you agree that it is highly unlikely that anyone from there was a customer of the defendant's?

I must. They had a big town with plenty of shops five miles away by road or rail. It would take them a couple of hours to get to us. Your client is welcome to trade there as far as I am concerned.

So you agree that it was not reasonably necessary, in order to protect the goodwill you acquired, to prevent the defendant from trading in those villages?

Yes. I never intended the clause to cover them.

CROSS-EXAMINATION

But it does, doesn't it?

I see that now.

As far as you know, did the business ever deal in china wall tiles or porcelain baths?

No.

Or plastic handbags, combs, toothbrushes?

No.

Or plastic billiard balls or tablecloths, or nylon shirts or socks?

No. I see what you're getting at—'goods made of plastic materials'. Does nylon fall under 'plastic materials'?

I shall lead evidence that it does. But if you're doubtful, forget about nylon for the moment. Think of the other things I've mentioned. You went much too far, didn't you?

To be honest, I must say that I did.

In the next example, the managing director of a company is being cross-examined about his summary dismissal of an employee. Under a relevant contract, he had the right to dismiss the plaintiff if he had reasonable grounds for believing that he had been guilty of dishonesty:

You didn't investigate the matter personally, did you?

I acted on the written report of the factory manager. I had legal advice that I was entitled to do that.

But you mean that you simply accepted the manager's finding?

No. I considered his facts, and on those facts I felt I had reasonable grounds for believing that the plaintiff was responsible for the theft of the money from the cash office.

What were those facts?

There were four points which influenced me. Firstly, his fingerprints were found in the cash office on the fourth floor, although he had no business there. He worked in Receiving and Dispatch on the ground floor. Do you want the other points now?

Yes, please. What were the other three?

Second. When he was told that he was suspected he immediately went red in the face and started blustering.

I must interrupt you. In what way did he bluster?

I don't know. But the manager is a careful, decent, responsible person. I've known him intimately since we were both boys. I can assure you that if he says the man blustered, he did bluster.

And the other two points?

When he was searched, they found on him two new banknotes which, according to the bank, had been issued to our firm the previous week. They would have gone to the cash office.

Yes, what else?

And those two notes were clipped together with an unusual sort of paper clip which we use in our pay offices. As far as I know you can't buy them in this country. I got them in Denmark.

Was your decision based on all these points, or some of them?

All of them. I knew what my duty was, and I did it. I considered the information as a whole, and in my honest opinion it was overwhelming.

You didn't think it was fair to ask the plaintiff for an explanation?

I was going to prosecute him; and I've always understood that the fair thing is not to question an accused person until he gives his evidence in court. The case against him was cast iron, anyhow. I resent your insinuation of unfairness.

Oh! Tell me, what would your reaction be if I suggested to you that you knew that the plaintiff was innocent, and that you'd trumped this up to protect your friend, the manager?

How dare you, sir! I won't stand this! You're lying … you're. ….. I don't know what to say! How dare you attack my integrity? I demand an apology. At once! Where's your evidence?

Bear with me, please. I have no evidence. And I do apologize for hurting your feelings. I have no reason whatever to suspect your honesty, or the manager's. But I wanted the court to see the reaction of an honest man to an unjust accusation. You went red in the face. And you blustered, didn't you?

Can you blame me?

CROSS-EXAMINATION

Can you blame the plaintiff if he went red in the face and blustered when the manager accused him of theft?

Perhaps I shouldn't have. But the other three points were enough.

When did the banknotes come from the bank?

According to them, on Thursday, the 6th.

Four days before the theft. Do you know whether the plaintiff drew any pay during those four days?

I don't know. But they are usually paid on Fridays.

Could he not have received those two notes as part of his pay on the Friday?

I don't know. The manager doesn't suggest it in his report.

And you did not consider that possibility, did you, when deciding whether you had reasonable grounds for believing that the plaintiff was a thief?

I'm afraid I overlooked it.

And if he did receive the notes in that way, might they not have been handed to him clipped together with the Danish paper clip?

Frankly, I think they would have been. But there's still the fingerprint in the cash office.

On what was it found?

A box of some sort. Let me see—the manager says it was a cardboard box containing envelopes.

Where does the factory get its envelopes?

From our stationers. We buy them in bulk.

And in what part of the building are they received?

I've never been present when they arrived; but they probably came to Receiving and Dispatch, I'll admit.

And you'll admit also that the plaintiff who handles incoming packages in that department, might well have put his fingerprints on the box there?

I can't say that he did. He may never have handled that box.

But he may have?

Yes.

What happens to your reasonable suspicions now?

I'd like to reconsider.

GEORGE COLMAN, Q.C.

To conclude this chapter, brief reference may be made to the use of practical tests in cross-examination. Elsewhere in this book there are indications of the manner in which the memory of a witness, or his knowledge of some subject, may be tested. The reference here is to specialized capacities of different kinds.

The appropriate method of testing will usually be suggested by the subject-matter. Nothing need be said about the manner in which counsel would test the ability of a witness to distinguish one type of wine from another, or to recognize the products of a particular textile mill. But there is something worth mentioning about the efforts which are frequently made to test the reliability of a time estimate which a witness has given, by asking him, in the courtroom, to estimate the duration of some interval or period. Such experiments are likely to produce misleading results. A person's subjective impression of the passage of time in the unfamiliar atmosphere of a courtroom is likely to differ greatly from the impressions he receives when about his normal business.

Nor is it always safe to rely upon a distance pointed out in the courtroom. If the witness is speaking of an indoor event, and the distance to be indicated is a short one, the demonstration may be fairly reliable. But a distance pointed out in the courtroom to represent a distance observed out of doors is likely to be misleading, for two reasons. One is that when the distance is a greater one than the room encloses, witnesses have a tendency, quite honestly, to select the furthest point in the room as the limit of the distance which they are seeking to indicate. The other is that distances indoors always appear, to untrained people, to be greater than the same distances appear in the open. Anyone who has looked at the foundations for a house to be built and later been inside the completed house will confirm that. If, therefore, a witness has pointed out a distance in the courtroom, and counsel believes that the true distance was substantially greater, he will have good prospects of making his point if he seeks and obtains an opportunity to ask the witness to indicate, out of doors, what the distance was.

CHAPTER VIII
EXPERTS

The term 'expert' is here used to mean a witness whose opinion on some matter is receivable in evidence because it is a matter upon which he is qualified by his special knowledge or experience to draw inferences and form views which the court cannot (or cannot so reliably) draw or express without the assistance of a person learned or experienced in the relevant field.

The question whether or not expert evidence is receivable on a particular point, and the question whether or not a particular witness is qualified to give such testimony, are governed by the law of evidence, and fall outside the scope of this book. It will be enough to say here that there is a wide range of persons who may be permitted to give expert evidence; some of them are highly qualified, others less so. And experts may testify upon a wide variety of subjects, some of which fall barely outside the court's own range of knowledge and experience, while others are so complicated or specialized that they can be understood by those unqualified in the relevant field only after elaborate and detailed exposition.

Ideally, counsel who has to cross-examine an expert will be assisted by experts of standing equal or superior to that of the witness to be cross-examined. Counsel will have had the benefit of conferences with the experts engaged by his own client; they will, as far as is necessary for his purpose, have explained the subject to him; they will have referred him to the relevant technical

GEORGE COLMAN, Q.C.

literature (if there is any) and helped him to understand it. If, as often happens, it was known what the witness was likely to say, the experts assisting counsel will possibly have pointed out flaws in his reasoning or uncertainties in his conclusions, and they will have pointed out lines of cross-examination which are likely to be useful. Often, these technical assistants to counsel will be able to tell him things about the witness himself which counsel may be able to use. And they will be at hand during the evidence in chief and the cross-examination to supplement this advice and to assist counsel in other ways.

But it is not always so. Sometimes the expert advice available to counsel comes from an adviser who is no match in knowledge, experience or intelligence, for the witness to be cross-examined. And sometimes counsel (because of the impecuniosity of his client or for other reasons) will have to cross-examine an expert without any technical assistance at all.

There are cases, of course, where there is little or no scope for cross-examination of an expert witness. If counsel's expert advisers tell him that, in their opinion, the testimony of the witness is well grounded, and his conclusions correct, there may be little or nothing to be achieved by cross-examination. But even in such a case, counsel should be alert, during the evidence for any opening which should be exploited on behalf of his client. The witness may phrase his conclusion, or one of the steps in his reasoning, in a manner which suggests to counsel that he has doubts or reservations which have not been raised by the advising experts, and a cautious examination of those doubts or reservations may be called for. For example:

> *Your words, Dr. White, were: 'I would say that the cause of death was a blow on the head.'*
>
> Yes.
>
> *That choice of words suggests that the post-mortem examination left you in some doubt about the cause of death. Is that what you intended to convey?*

CROSS-EXAMINATION

That could call forth the answer:

> No. I did not have any doubt, and I did not intend to express any.

That may end the matter, and if so, no harm has been done. Or counsel, if he has grounds for believing that the answer was not candid, and that he has prospects of showing it, may press his question further, calling upon the witness to justify his use of the phrase 'I would say'. But the original approach may elicit a more favourable answer, such as this one:

> I used the phrase 'I would say' because there were some features which one does not usually expect in a case where death is caused by a head injury.

And that will open up a legitimate and prospectively helpful inquiry into the possibility that death was caused by something else. It is unlikely that the witness will commit himself to the opinion that the other hypothetical cause was probably the operative one. He has already expressed the view that, in spite of the unusual features found by him, the cause of death was a blow on the head. But he might be induced to depart from that view if given facts not previously available to him, such as the fact, or the probability, that the deceased had suffered from some disease which had not shown itself in the autopsy. And even if that result cannot be achieved, further cross-examination may be useful in clarifying the extent of the witness's doubts, and hence the strength with which his opinion is held, and the weight which can properly be given to it.

It is appropriate here to say something about probabilities in relation to expert evidence: What an expert deposes to is often (though not always) opinion, as opposed to fact. And however competent and honest the witness may be, it is often useful to ascertain the degree of confidence with which his opinion is held. Lawyers are familiar with the degrees of probability required to discharge burdens of proof; in a criminal case proof beyond reasonable doubt

GEORGE COLMAN, Q.C.

is required of the prosecution; in a civil case a substantial preponderance of probabilities will normally (if not always) suffice. But expert witnesses are not always familiar with these crude, but useful yardsticks. When a handwriting expert says:

> In my opinion this document was written by the person who wrote up the cash-book you have shown me,

he may mean either that he has no doubt whatsoever on the point, or that he is very hesitantly inclined to that view. Or he may mean something between those two extremes. It may be appropriate for counsel to seek clarification about that, and it is not always easy to obtain it, even from a candid witness who is trying to assist the court. The witness, unfamiliar with legal concepts, may not understand fully what is meant by 'reasonable doubt' or 'substantial preponderance of probability'. Some experts in seeking to convey their states of mind, resort to figures, but that is not always helpful. The answer 'I am 99.9 per cent certain' is, perhaps, clear enough for most purposes. But 'I am 55 per cent to 60 per cent sure' may not be. A technique which is sometimes useful in such a case is to ask the witness to indicate how willing he would be to act upon his belief in some hypothetical situation. Thus, of an architect who has said 'I am reasonably sure that the floor was safe' one might seek clarification by asking—

> *Would you have advised a headmistress that it was safe to hold a school dance on the floor?*

To a neurologist who has said 'I consider it unlikely that the plaintiff will have another fainting fit', this question might be put—

> *If he was a qualified pilot, would you travel in an aircraft piloted by him?*

or, less dramatically—

CROSS-EXAMINATION

*Would you advise him to undertake an occupation in which he will work
at the top of high ladders?*

Of the expert whose evidence in chief is incontestable, this can
be added: Counsel should bear in mind the possibility that cross-
examination may elicit something helpful to his case on an issue
unrelated to the evidence in chief. It may be that in a widow's suit
for damages arising out of a collision, a pathologist has testified to
post-mortem findings which show, indisputably, that the man died
as a result of the collision. Counsel, while unable usefully to cross-
examine about the cause of death, may help to mitigate the damages by cross-examining along these lines:

What was the state of his heart, doctor?
His death was unconnected with his heart. As I've said, he died
    of a laceration of his brain.
But it was your duty to examine all the vital organs, was it not?
Yes, and I did.
What was the state of his heart?
There was some enlargement.

Further questions might elicit the unlikelihood that the husband
would have been able to continue the support of his family for many
years, even if he had not been involved in an accident.

Similarly, if, in a matrimonial case, the family doctor has been
called to speak of an occasion when he had to attend to wounds
inflicted upon the wife by her husband, counsel for the husband
may be able to draw from him, as a regular attendant on the family
and a regular visitor at its home, information about the wife's habits
and temperament which will be useful to her husband's case.

Similar opportunities can arise in criminal cases. In an embez-
zlement case an auditor has proved that the accused defrauded the
firm by which he was employed as a junior clerk. Defending counsel
may find it impossible to challenge this evidence. But he might be
able, in cross-examining the auditor, to elicit evidence which will

GEORGE COLMAN, Q.C.

be useful in mitigation of sentence. He may, for example, be able to show, out of the auditor's mouth, that the accounting system of the firm was such that the accused was laid open to great temptation. Or he may be able to extract the information that the accused was grossly underpaid, and must have been having a hard struggle to support himself.

As a final illustration on this point one can take a claim under a fire insurance policy. On behalf of the plaintiff an expert has expressed the opinion, based on his inspection of the burnt-out premises, that the fire arose in a manner covered by the terms of the relevant policy. Counsel, even if he is unable usefully to attack this finding, may be able to extract from the witness evidence which shows, or helps to show, that the insured has committed a breach of some warranty which appears in the policy, such as a warranty that the books of account would be kept in a fireproof safe, a warranty that no inflammable fluids be kept on the premises, or a warranty that no structural alterations would be made to the premises during the currency of the policy.

We turn now to the expert whose evidence in chief is in dispute, so that the aim of the cross-examiner is to break it down or weaken it. Usually, in such a case, counsel will have called, or will be about to call, one or more expert witnesses to give evidence which differs from that of the expert to be cross-examined: his aim, then, will be to persuade the court either to reject the evidence of that witness, or to prefer the views of those who differ from him. Competent cross-examination may well bring about such a result.

The main considerations to be borne in mind by counsel are these: Those who profess expert knowledge do not always command it; and those who command it are not always right; a man who is well qualified in a broad field may not know anything, or may not know a great deal, about the narrow question in issue in the case; often the state of knowledge in the relevant field is subject to more uncertainty than appears from the expert's evidence in chief; his knowledge may be out of date; there may be flaws in his reasoning. It is not uncommon that the witness has been given, or

CROSS-EXAMINATION

has assumed for the purposes of his findings, data which are incorrect, or are open to doubt. It may be that the expert is seeking, wilfully, to mislead the court; motives for doing so, such as friendship with, loyalty to, or sympathy for the litigant who has called him, may be present; the attractive prospect of lucrative employment as an expert in similar cases may also play a part.

More frequently the expert is a victim of the unconscious bias from which few who find themselves concerned in litigation are wholly free. The heat of a contest tends to kindle the glow of partisanship in the unconscious minds even of people who have nothing to gain or lose by the outcome, and who would not consciously favour one litigant at the expense of the other. When the litigant on whose behalf the expert has been called is an attractive person, one whose condition or circumstances call for sympathy, or one to whom failure in the suit would be disastrous, the danger of unconscious partisanship may be great. Professional rivalry between experts may likewise give rise to bias and distortion, conscious or unconscious; nor is it uncommon that the views of an expert are coloured by some strongly held theory or approach of his own which is not shared by any, or by the majority of his colleagues. Vanity, too, may colour the testimony of an expert, as, indeed, of any witness; in particular, he may find it humiliating to admit that something which he has said, in or out of court, was wrong, and he may (perhaps unconsciously) try to avoid making the admission unless offered an opportunity of doing so in a way which will save his face.

All these things the cross-examiner should bear in mind when he approaches the task of cross-examining an expert. There will, later in this chapter, be illustrations of the manner in which some of these possible situations can be revealed or dealt with. But it should be understood that most of the examples will necessarily be over-simplified. In relation to expert evidence, particularly, it has been found impracticable to make the examples realistic. Often the record of the thorough cross-examination of an expert is lengthier than the whole of this book. And it is seldom that counsel can hope for the quick successes which the examples embody. Yet it can be

GEORGE COLMAN, Q.C.

hoped that they will be helpful pointers to what can be achieved in practice.

In these illustrations, it will be found, the technical field most often chosen is that of medicine. That is not only because medical witnesses testify more frequently than experts in other fields. Another reason is that the broad nature of the problems with which such witnesses deal can be understood without such lengthy exposition as would be required to render intelligible examples taken from less familiar fields. But the techniques illustrated are, in most cases, applicable to the cross-examination of experts of all kinds.

In considering the cross-examination of an expert counsel will, of course, bear in mind what appears elsewhere in this book about witnesses in general; but experts present special difficulties even if counsel has able technical assistance. For this sort of cross-examination, perhaps more than any other, thorough preparation is important; for counsel, whose education, experience and knowledge of human affairs gives him an advantage over the average non-technical witness, here starts from an inferior position. Without a proper knowledge and understanding of the relevant material he may be unable to detect fallacies, unable to cope with evasions, and unable to expose exaggerations and distortions.

Yet the task, with suitable assistance, of qualifying himself to cross-examine competently, even in a field unfamiliar to counsel, is not so formidable as, on the face of it, one might think. All human knowledge is capable of formulation in propositions which an educated man, having taken sufficient trouble, can understand. Anything which is not patient of such formulation is not knowledge which a court should accept as a basis for its findings: and cross-examining counsel is justified in requiring of an expert witness that he expound his reasoning in such intelligible propositions as the court can follow.

There are cases in which counsel is forced to pick up his knowledge of the technical principles from the witness as his cross-examination develops. But if he is driven to that, he is at a disadvantage. If it is in any way possible, he should be instructed,

CROSS-EXAMINATION

or should instruct himself, in advance; and there are cases in which he is justified in asking the court to give him time, after some of the expert's evidence has been given, to qualify himself for cross-examination, or further cross-examination, as the case may be.

In the course of such preparation hard work and clear thought will usually bring the relevant problem or problems within a manageable ambit, and thus place counsel on substantially equal terms with the witness. The field of chemistry is vast: but it is not difficult for counsel to equip himself to test, competently, the evidence of an expert who claims to have established, by chemical analysis, that the stains on a shirt consist of human blood. Nor is an understanding of the full range of mechanical engineering required by counsel whose task it is to cross-examine on the question whether the unsatisfactory performance of a printing press is due to defects in its manufacture or to misuse by its owner. Having conferred with an expert, examined a few printing presses and their components, seen some drawings, and observed some printers at work, he will almost certainly be equal to the task. On other subjects the preparation may be more arduous, especially if literature requires to be studied, and technical terms mastered.

Clear sketches are often an aid, not only to the understanding of technical problems, but also to their investigation in the course of cross-examination. Even more so is this true, in some cases, of models and simulacra. If counsel feels that these will be useful, and the necessary funds are available, he should cause them to be made. Photographs, too, can be useful, and in fingerprint and handwriting cases photographic enlargements are almost indispensable; but they will normally be provided by the litigant who calls the expert witness to be cross-examined.

When counsel is considering his approach to the cross-examination of a witness put forward as an expert, his attention should be directed, firstly, to the question whether the witness is really qualified to give expert evidence on the matter in issue, and secondly (if the witness is so qualified to the extent that his evidence is receivable), to the question whether his knowledge and

GEORGE COLMAN, Q.C.

experience are sufficient to justify the court in accepting his views on the specific problem to which his testimony relates. The witness will, in his evidence in chief, testify to his qualifications, and that testimony, normally, will establish, prima facie, that he has qualifications in the relevant field which justify the court in receiving opinion evidence from him.

But cross-examination may show that the witness does not really possess the necessary knowledge and experience. It will be for counsel to decide whether to wait until the evidence in chief has been given before he seeks to expose such a lack of qualification; an alternative course (and generally the preferable one before a jury or other tribunal not legally qualified) is to seek an opportunity to test the qualifications of the witness before he is allowed to express any opinions.

The type of cross-examination referred to is illustrated in the following examples:

You have told us that you are a watchmaker of forty years' experience?
Yes.
And during thirty of those years you have conducted a suburban watchmaker's establishment?
Yes.
Dealing with ordinary wrist-watches and pocket-watches?
I would say all kinds of wrist-watches and pocket-watches; and clocks, too.
All kinds of clocks?
Well, I've never had to do with a clock like the one this case is about. But they all work on the same principles.
We are dealing here with a large clock installed in the tower of a church, are we not?
Yes.
And the question is whether it failed because of one of its parts couldn't stand up to weather conditions?
I understand so.
You have had no experience of that sort of difficulty?

CROSS-EXAMINATION

Well, not with clocks.

Not with anything, as an expert?

No.

You were taught nothing about that during your apprenticeship?

I was taught what rust can do to the moving parts of a clock.

But not about the materials which are needed to stand up to weather in an outdoor clock? Or how to protect those materials?

No.

In fact you have no knowledge or experience about those matters?

Well, I tried to read it up in the public library.

But without much success, may I suggest?

Well, I found something which I think may help in a book on metallurgy.

You say you think it may help because you found it a little hard to understand?

Yes.

You are not a qualified metallurgist?

No.

You really have no training in, or knowledge or experience of that subject, have you?

No. I know as much as the average man.

And this is a metallurgical problem, isn't it?

I think I must agree with that.

Or, within a narrower compass, an actuary might be questioned along these lines upon one of the points he has made in testifying about the compensation which should be awarded to a widow for the loss of support consequent upon the death of her husband:

You have allowed 30 per cent for her prospects of remarriage. Why 30 per cent?

That is what is normally allowed for a childless widow of her age; there are statistics to support it.

Had you seen the plaintiff before making your calculations?

No.

GEORGE COLMAN, Q.C.

Now that you have seen her in court, will you agree that she is unusually good looking?

Yes.

I will ask you to accept, also, that she is a gay, witty person, good at games, and able to make friends easily. Also that she is a qualified nurse.

Yes.

She has lived all her life in a copper-mining area. Now are you capable of assessing the prospects of remarriage, in a copper-mining area, of a pretty, gay, witty, popular young woman like the plaintiff, who also has professional qualifications?

That's rather difficult.

You have no statistics or professional experience which will answer that question for you, have you?

No.

So on that point the court cannot treat you as an expert, can it?

No.

With almost any type of expert the situation can arise that in reply to—

How do you know that?

the answer is—

Because my common sense tells me so.

And on that matter it can sometimes be argued (although much depends on the context) that the witness was not really speaking as an expert, and cannot be treated as such.

More common than the case in which it is possible to take all or part of the testimony of a witness out of the category of expert evidence, is the case in which appropriate questions about his knowledge and experience will reduce the weight of his evidence. Thus—

CROSS-EXAMINATION

The disease of which you are speaking, doctor, is fairly rare in this country, is it not?

Yes.

How many cases have you seen in the course of your practice?

I can remember one only before this one. But I saw a few at medical school.

Forty years ago or more?

Thirty-nine, to be exact.

And I don't suppose that in the course of a busy practice you've found the time to do much reading on it?

No. But I've read all I could find during the past few weeks. I'm afraid it wasn't very helpful.

Do you know Dr. White, whom I shall be calling as a witness?

No.

He practised for twenty years in Burma, where the disease is common. He treated over a hundred cases of it. Would you agree that he is better qualified to speak of it than you?

Of course, if that is his experience.

That was a modest and compliant witness. Counsel might have more difficulty with a witness who answers the question about his reading differently:

I've always been interested in the disease, and I've read all there is to read about it. I think that makes up for my lack of practical experience.

Is reading ever a complete substitute for clinical experience?

It's far more important. You can't learn much from a few cases. My reading has equipped me with the accumulated knowledge of the world on this subject.

The world, doctor? You read Russian?

No. But I don't think they know much about this condition there.

Have you read the German and Spanish literature? Do you follow the Dutch medical journals?

Perhaps I should have said 'the English-speaking world'.

GEORGE COLMAN, Q.C.

Perhaps. Would you be good enough to mention the names of a few of the recent publications on this subject which you have studied?

Well, there's a paper by White, and one by Black; there's a passage in Green's book which has some bearing. ...

Any others, doctor?

Those are the main ones. There are others.

I take it that the authorities which you have mentioned support your view?

The first two clearly do. The third doesn't seem to; but on analysis you'll find that it really does.

Can I take it that there are other recent authorities which are against your view?

I suppose you mean Brown.

Well, isn't Brown the leading authority in this branch of medicine?

He thinks he is.

Do not others think so too?

I don't know.

Pink is a recognized authority on the subject, is he not?

Yes, I suppose he is.

Does not Professor Pink refer to Brown's paper as the most important contribution to the subject in this century?

I don't remember. If he said that he was wrong.

Does the latest edition of Blue's book deal with the problem?

I think so. Yes, I remember looking at it before I wrote my report. I wasn't impressed.

Before you wrote your report, doctor? But it was only published after you signed your report.

Then I must have been mistaken. Perhaps it was after.

Did he support your view?

I don't remember.

Did he refer to any cases not previously reported?

I don't remember.

And you are here giving the court the benefit of the accumulated knowledge of the world on the subject?

I'm giving my view, based on what convinces me.

CROSS-EXAMINATION

The opinion of this witness may ultimately be accepted. But it will probably be approached more cautiously than it would have been but for these questions and answers. He will, of course, be cross-examined further, but this much will suffice for the present example.

It remains to be added, on this type of cross-examination, that many an expert is fully qualified to express the opinion which he does express. The more he is asked about his knowledge and experience, the more apparent that is likely to become.

With such a witness it may prove fruitful to examine the data relied upon. Experts often rely upon their own observations. But equally often their conclusions rest wholly, or in part, upon data presented to them. It may be necessary to inquire into the source of the data, and into the effect it would have upon the conclusion if some of them were incorrect, or incapable of proof.

Thus, of a valuer of immovable property whose valuation is in dispute, a useful question is—

What information did you have before you when you valued this block of flats and shops?

The witness will no doubt give, in reply, a list of data relating to the property, its physical features, what it cost, the rents it yields, and the prices fetched by comparable properties in the neighbourhood; he may refer to the potentialities for adding further floors, or increasing rentals. He may mention such matters as the scarcity of accommodation in the area, the growing demand for income-yielding buildings as investments, or the flourishing state of business. It may be well to ask him if that was all he relied upon, and then to inquire from whom certain of the data were obtained. Something of this sort may follow:

You speak of the possibility of adding two further floors of flats?
Yes.
Did you regard that as important?

GEORGE COLMAN, Q.C.

Well, it will add 20 per cent to the net yield.
So but for that your figure would have been lower?
Certainly.
By how much?

(An approximate figure is given.)

Who told you that the foundations would support another two storeys?
The present owner.
But he is a greengrocer, not an architect?
I assumed that he knew what he was talking about.
You made no effort to verify his statement?
No, but I should think he was right.
Are you an architect or a structural engineer?
No.
You don't really know, do you, whether the extra floors are technically possible?
No.
And if they are not, your valuation is wrong?
I've valued conservatively.
If you had thought that the two further floors were impossible your valuation would have been a good deal lower?
Yes.
Who gave you the rentals?
The letting agent.
Did you ask him whether there was any difficulty in getting them?
He said there wasn't.
Did you know that three of the shops stood empty for over a year because no one would hire them?
No.
Did you know that some of the flat tenants are leaving?
No.
Did you know that flats in the new building across the road are being offered for lower rents?
No. I don't see why that should be. From my experience I should say that that was unlikely. They are better flats.

CROSS-EXAMINATION

That's why I didn't inquire.

You knew that most of the tenants in this neighbourhood work in the soap factory?

Yes.

You didn't know that the soap factory is about to close down?

No.

If you had been told all these things your valuation would have been much lower?

The following example relates to the evidence of an expert who has deposed to the nature and extent of the impurities in water released from a factory:

Your opinion is based on samples taken at intervals of three hours over a period of ten days?

Yes.

Did you analyse the samples yourself?

They were analysed under my supervision.

By whom?

By three of my assistants.

Did you watch each of them carry out each analysis from start to finish?

No. I couldn't possibly spare the time to do that.

So you cannot swear that the somewhat complicated process was correctly carried out?

I can't swear to it, but I'd be surprised if my assistants made mistakes.

If they did, your conclusion may be wrong?

Yes.

Did you take the samples yourself?

I've told you, I'm a busy man. I couldn't sit for ten days at the sewer outlet of the defendant's factory.

Who took the samples?

One of the defendant's officials.

Should it not have been an independent person?

I have no reason to think that the official was dishonest.

GEORGE COLMAN, Q.C.

I don't say he was. But this case is of vital importance to his employer, and if he was dishonest he could have diluted the samples, could he not?
He could have.
And if he did your findings are valueless?
If he did, yes.
What was to stop the factory from releasing its worst effluent between the three-hourly samplings?
I suppose they could have managed to do that.
It would have been a more reliable test if an independent person had come and taken samples, without warning, at irregular intervals.
Do you agree?
I'm not as suspicious as you are.
That is no answer to my question. Do you agree with the suggestion I made?
If the defendant and its officials were honest and didn't deliberately regulate the effluent so as to get a favourable result, there's nothing wrong with my procedure.
If not?
Then, I must admit, my figures may be misleading.

If the expert's assistants and the employees of the factory are called, and their evidence persuades the court that counsel's suggestions were ill founded, the effect of this cross-examination will be negative. But this may not happen. What counsel has achieved is to show that what, on the face of it, was the finding of an independent and highly qualified expert was in truth a finding dependent on the conduct of others, some of whom were by no means disinterested.

With a medical witness, a similar approach can be useful. Here is an example:

In reaching your diagnosis of the plaintiff's condition, have you relied on all the symptoms which you have mentioned?
Yes.
Of those, the headaches and the dizz y spells are important?
Very important.

CROSS-EXAMINATION

You never saw him in one of the dizz y spells, did you?

No.

And apart from his own statement there is no way of telling whether he has them or not?

No. There are no tests for that.

Nor can you, apart from what the plaintiff tells you, say whether he has headaches, or if he does, how severe they are?

No. But I have no reason to disbelieve my patient.

Perhaps not. But the court will see him and hear him being cross-examined. What if the court is of the opinion that he is exaggerating his symptoms?

In that event it would be unsafe to accept my diagnosis.

If the data which the expert has relied upon, and his qualifications are well established, the cross-examination must be directed to the soundness of his reasoning and the validity of his conclusion. Here it is usually necessary to take the witness through his mental processes, step by step. Typical questions which may have to be asked, and if necessary, pressed, are such as these:

What does that term mean, in simple language?

Why do you draw that inference?

Have you any authorities which support that view?

Could that not have been due to...?

Is it not reasonably possible that...?

How do you know that?

Why should that be?

Does not the presence of... tend to weaken your theory?

If the witness has previously said something inconsistent with, or tending to weaken his present evidence, that should be put to him, but it will sometimes be wise to spare him the embarrassment attendant upon self-contradiction by some such means as these:

Many months have gone by since you performed the operation?

GEORGE COLMAN, Q.C.

Yes.

Can I take it that you have performed many similar operations since?

Yes.

So naturally your impressions of what you saw then were more vivid when you wrote your original report than they are now?

A little; but I still remember the operation pretty well.

I've asked the question because here you've said that there were a number of substantial cracks in the bone. Your report uses these words 'one or two hairline cracks'. Now that I've refreshed your memory, would you say that that describes more accurately what you saw?

Conversely, when counsel is seeking an answer which differs from what the witness has previously said, he might see fit to lay the foundation thus:

Before writing your letter you had only tested the machine hurriedly?

Yes.

Since then you've made fuller tests?

Yes.

And in the course of these proceedings you have heard things about the behaviour of the machine which you could not have known before?

I have.

Assuming that the evidence you have heard is truthful, would you agree that the defects are more serious than you originally thought?

The evidence to be given by experts who hold conflicting views must be put in cross-examination. And this relates not merely to their conclusions, but to what they will say they observed, and their reasoning. The witness should be required to say, on each material point, whether he disagrees, and if so, why. His reasoning can then be examined more closely, and he might be invited to say whether there is not, at any rate, a reasonable possibility that the opposing view is correct. If he makes that concession, it may be very useful. If he refuses to do so in a manner which suggests to the court that he is obstinate or unduly dogmatic, that may be helpful to the cross-examiner's case.

CROSS-EXAMINATION

Authorities which conflict with the evidence of the witness should be put to him. He should be asked, first, to acknowledge the authoritative nature of the work to be relied upon. If he does, the relevant passage may be put to him. If he does not, he may be told that other experts will say that the work is authoritative and then be asked to deal with what the writer says.

When counsel has an authority available to him which clearly and strongly supports some aspect of his case, he may find it necessary to choose between one of two approaches, the choice being dependent upon the circumstances, and his assessment of the witness. He may think it desirable to reveal his authority to the witness before the latter has committed himself, or committed himself too deeply, upon the specific point, so as to make it easier for the witness, if he is so disposed, to agree with the writer, or to disagree with reservations. In another case, more particularly when the aim is to discredit the witness generally, counsel will draw the witness out fully on the point in issue, let him commit himself fully, and then produce his authority.

Usually, in making use of a technical work, counsel should do more than put to the witness the conclusion of the writer. It will be better to use that conclusion in its context. A passage of appropriate length is selected, and put to the witness, sentence by sentence, thus:

Now that you have agreed that this is an accepted authority, I shall ask for your comments on a passage in it. It begins on page 142, with these words: 'The test commonly used is the diluted acid test.' Do you agree with that?

Yes. That is the test I've relied upon.

That is all you relied upon, isn't it?

It's all I could rely on. If that book mentions any other test I'll be surprised.

And on the basis of the diluted acid test you convinced yourself beyond doubt of the composition of the sample?

Beyond any reasonable doubt.

GEORGE COLMAN, Q.C.

You have no substantial doubt?

That's what I've just said.

You will see why I chose the word 'substantial' when I read you the next sentence from the book: 'The validity of that test is, however, open to substantial doubts' Do you agree?

I'm afraid not. I don't know why he says that.

I'll read on: 'Although, for many years it appeared to yield consistent and reliable results, recent studies in Scandinavia have thrown up serious anomalies' Are you familiar with the Scandinavian studies?

No. Can you tell me what they showed?

The results are shown in Figures 100 *and Table* 100A. *Look at them please? (Pause)—What do you say now?*

This surprises me, but I don't think it justifies me in regarding the test as unreliable.

It doesn't raise any doubts in your mind at all?

I won't say that. Of course, this sort of thing, in a book of this importance, raises some doubts. But, on the whole, I think the diluted acid test is still fairly reliable.

Hand the book back please. I'll now read to you from page 144: *'But what is even more significant is the discovery by Mauve who, in following up the results of the Scandinavian studies, found, in* 17 *cases that the test, repeated after three days on the same material, gave a reading which diverged by more than* 34 *per cent from the original one.' May I have your comment?*

Well, I don't really know what to say.

Perhaps you will say, in the words of this book, that 'In the circumstances it is dangerous to place reliance upon the diluted acid test'. Are you able to assure the court that that proposition is unsound?

At the core of an expert's reasoning there often lies an inference, or an exercise of judgment, which is open to criticism. The cross-examiner's aim will be, firstly, to work his way with the witness through the technicalities and surrounding details until it has become plain what the critical point is, and what influence the expert's approach to it has had (or should have had) upon his conclusion. Having achieved that, counsel will show, if he can, that the

CROSS-EXAMINATION

inference is unjustified, or open to doubt, or that the expert's judgment was not soundly exercised.

In a case about a collision between an electric tram-car and another vehicle, the tram-driver will say that his brakes did not function as they should have done at the critical stage. An expert is called by the other side to say that he examined the tram and found its brakes to be in order, so that a competent driver would have been able (at the relevant speed) to stop it within twenty-seven yards. Here are some of the questions which may be put to the expert, and his possible replies:

You have stressed the fact that there were three independent brakes available for the driver to use?

Yes, and in addition, if he had put the tram into reverse, that would have had a braking effect.

So you are suggesting that there were four things which he could have done to stop the vehicle?

Yes.

Each process involved a different manual movement, and the use of a different handle or lever?

Yes.

Are you suggesting that he could have used all four?

That depends upon how much time he had.

Are you familiar with the circumstances of the collision?

I know roughly what happened.

I must ask you to assume, when answering my next few questions, that the driver had, at most, two and a half seconds after the danger became apparent, to deal with it.

Yes, I'll assume that.

Was one of the brakes a mechanical one which one applies by turning a handle round and round?

Yes.

And it would have taken several turns of the handle to bring the tram to a stop?

Yes.

143

GEORGE COLMAN, Q.C.

Our tests show that that cannot be done in two and a half seconds. Do you agree?

I haven't timed it.

Then you cannot dispute what I say?

No.

So we can leave the mechanical brake out of our considerations?

I suppose so. It's not really an emergency brake.

Which is the emergency brake?

There are two. One is the short brass lever which works the power brakes on the wheels. A quite simple movement applies it and it operates at once.

We'll call that the wheel brake. Which is the other, and how does it work?

The long iron lever. When you pull it towards you two bars come down on the tracks and there is a powerful magnetic attraction between the bars and the tracks.

Is that what you call the magnetic brake?

Yes.

So that is dependent on the electrical power supply through the overhead wire?

Well, there's a bit of braking power through friction. But the main effectiveness is dependent on the power supply.

And that applies to the wheel brake too?

Yes.

And the reversing mechanism?

That also works on the electrical power.

So three of your four braking processes are not really independent, are they?

They are mechanically independent. If one of them jammed, or if a rod snapped in one of the mechanisms, the other would still work. And it would only take a second or so to apply all three.

But if the power failed, all three would be useless, would they not?

If the power failed. But when there's a power failure tram-cars stop all over the city, and we know all about it. Nothing like that happened on the day of this collision.

CROSS-EXAMINATION

Can there not be an interruption in the supply of power which lasts for something between one and one and a half seconds?

I've never heard of such a thing.

I have an expert who will say that it can and does happen. He will say. ...

Here follows a technical explanation and a series of questions and answers after which the witness says:

Well, I'll accept that such a thing may happen.

If it does, the tram-cars in motion will not stop. Their momentum will carry them on, will it not?

Yes, but the drivers, I should think, would notice a slight check in speed.

That's not the sort of thing a driver would report, or even remember, would he?

Perhaps not, unless it happened often.

So if it happened at the time of this accident you would not know of it, would you?

Not necessarily, I suppose.

And if it happened at the critical moment, the driver had no effective emergency brakes?

Yes. But that's too much of a coincidence.

What do you mean by a coincidence?

Well, I mean it's unlikely that that would happen just at the time of the collision.

But if there's a causal connection between the power interruption and the collision, you can't call that a coincidence, can you?

That's a bit too deep for me.

If, without looking, I fire a single bullet at random into the air, and it happens to hit the only bird that's flying in the area, that's a coincidence, isn't it?

Yes.

But if I fire fifty bullets into the air on a number of days when there are hundreds of birds about, and one day I hit one bird, that's not what we call a coincidence, is it?

145

I suppose not.

There may, last year, have been a dozen momentary power failures, affecting hundreds of tram-cars. Is there anything unacceptable about the suggestion that one of them happened to affect one tram-car at the moment when the driver needed his emergency brakes?

I see what you mean.

It may have happened, may it not?

It may.

Or the cross-examination of a valuer who has deposed to the market value of an income-yielding investment may conclude in this way:

So it comes down to this. Your valuation is entirely dependent upon the proposition that at that time an investor would have required a return of at least 9 per cent per annum on his outlay in an investment of this sort?

Yes.

And if I can satisfy the court that there were many investors then looking for investments of this kind who would have been content with 7 per cent per annum, you will agree that your figure cannot be accepted?

It would surprise me if you could prove that. But if you can, my valuation is wrong.

This chapter will conclude with a longer simplified example of the cross-examination of an expert in which, it is hoped, the reader will find helpful illustrations of some of the points which have been mentioned in the text.

The example is taken from a hypothetical defamation case. The defendant has published, over his own name, a number of articles in which he took part in a political controversy. Soon after that, a pamphlet signed CITIZEN has been distributed. The pamphlet supports the political contentions of the defendant, and in it there is a passage seriously libellous of the plaintiff. The defendant has denied that he wrote the pamphlet, but the plaintiff has called a

CROSS-EXAMINATION

professor of English literature to express the view, based on the style of the pamphlet, that the defendant was its author.

Is this not a somewhat unusual role in which you find yourself, Professor? I mean the role of an expert witness?

I've never given evidence before, but I've been a student of prose style for forty years.

I'm not reflecting on your competence as a professor or a critic. But do you really claim the ability to say, on the basis of style alone, who the author is of a piece of prose?

I've not made so wide a claim. My position is roughly this: in some cases there are stylistic traits which identify the author. A man may leave his personal mark on his writings as clearly as he leaves his fingerprints on what he touches.

But sometimes the fingerprints are blurred, are they not?

Oh, yes. But not, I thought, in this case.

Is your opinion based solely upon the four stylistic mannerisms, as you call them, which you have mentioned in your evidence in chief?

Not solely. There's a general distinctive quality which is common to the pamphlet and your client's signed article.

Would you please be a little more specific?

I'm afraid I can't. It's an elusive thing, which I can't put into words. Perhaps it's of the nature of a subtle prose rhythm.

It's there, but it defies analysis.

Well, I don't think the court is going to award damages against the defendant on the basis of an elusive quality which defies analysis and can't be put into words; so I shan't trouble you further on that. Was there anything else?

Well, the political position taken up by the writer of the pamphlet seems to me to be similar to the defendant's.

You don't claim to be an expert on politics, do you?

Certainly not.

Then we'll leave that to the court. By the way, what are your politics, Professor?

That is an impertinent question.

147

GEORGE COLMAN, Q.C.

What are your politics?

Are you imputing dishonesty to me?

No. But I want the court to know what your politics are. What are they?

It will take a long time to give you all my political beliefs.

Why the reluctance, Professor? Are you a supporter of the Government or not?

I am not. My political position is close to that of the Opposition.

I take it, then, that you disapprove of the defendant's articles?

Well, seeing you ask me, I'll say that in my view they are subversive rubbish, and so is the pamphlet.

In broad terms, what would you say of the defendant's prose style?

It's a good style. The style, I would say, of a well-educated sensitive writer. But he has mannerisms. Some of them, by the way, show the influence of a Scottish environment. That is of some importance, because they are particularly marked in the pamphlet, and I understand that the defendant was educated in Glasgow.

He has never been in Scotland in his life, Professor. Are you sure that you see Scottish influences?

I wasn't suggesting that they were strongly marked, but I think I detected something like that.

You think you saw something like that. That's not how you put it before, is it?

Perhaps not. But it's not a point which weighed much with me.

Presumably what we might call the 'Scottish mannerisms' were picked up by the defendant in his reading of Scottish writers?

That must have been so, if he was never in Scotland.

Tell me now about the first of the four stylistic mannerisms you mentioned in chief. It is the frequent use of the phrase 'Let us now consider'. Is that not a perfectly normal expression?

Yes. But it appears with unusual frequency in your client's articles; and in the pamphlet of CITIZEN I find the same frequency. It's a mannerism, and to me a significant one, taken in conjunction with the other similarities.

The next mannerism is the use of the word 'germane'?

CROSS-EXAMINATION

Yes. That one is very important. It's a perfectly good word. And it's aptly used. But it's used often in the articles and the pamphlet. And in a search of all the recent political writings and speeches published here which I could lay hands on, I found no one else who was using it at all. They all say, 'relevant' or 'in point' or 'bearing upon'.

Is it fair, having regard to the subject matter, to assume that CITIZEN, *if he was not the defendant, had read the defendant's articles before he wrote his pamphlet?*

There is no internal evidence that he did. But he may have.

And if he did read them, and he admired them, is there any relevant possibility that occurs to you?

Do you mean that he has aped them?

No. But you have said that the defendant may have picked up Scottish mannerisms from reading Scottish writers. Is it not probable that CITIZEN, *when he saw the apt but neglected word 'germane' in the defendant's articles, was attracted by it, and adopted it, consciously or unconsciously?*

As you know, I visualize one author, not two. But if there were two, then that could have happened.

And something similar could have happened with the expression 'Let us now consider'? It could have. *And the use in the pamphlet of the other two of the defendant's stylistic mannerisms could be similarly explained?*

Only if CITIZEN was deeply impressed by the defendant's articles, and, I would say, read them several times.

Perhaps he did?

Perhaps he did.

Let me draw your attention to another expression which appears often in the articles. The defendant, when dealing with the approach of the Government to various problems, often says 'the Government's position' is this or that. Did you notice that?

Yes. It's a metaphor.

And a stylistic mannerism?

GEORGE COLMAN, Q.C.

Yes. But it's of no importance that it doesn't happen to appear in the pamphlet.

You aren't CITIZEN, *are you?*

Certainly not.

Would it surprise you to hear that on two or three occasions this morning, when explaining your views, you have referred to your 'position'?

I wasn't conscious of it. I may have.

So it's easy to pick up a stylistic mannerism?

I suppose we all do it. I've spent many weary hours with these articles lately.

During that time were you alert for negative indications? You know what I mean?

Yes, I was. I found none.

Let me help you. In the pamphlet, on page 4, you will see the expression 'the tender mercies of officialdom'.

Yes.

A hackneyed phrase, I suggest, which no good writer would use today?

Yes, it's well below the defendant's normal level.

And on the same page CITIZEN *says that something 'centres round the budget'. Is that not a bad phrase?*

It's a barbarism. I overlooked it, and I must grant you that it's surprising to find the defendant using it, if it was he who did.

You are developing doubts, Professor?

That's putting it a little strongly.

A shade of doubt?

I'll have to concede you that.

Did you compare CITIZEN'S *punctuation with the defendant's?*

No. You don't find many mannerisms in punctuation.

Some people use colons freely, others hardly at all?

That is true.

I have counted 27 colons in the pamphlet, and I can't find more than one in the articles. I fully understand that you didn't go into that. But if you had found that, would you have put forward your view quite so confidently? It's a point; not a very strong one in my view. Please answer my question.

Not quite so confidently.

Look, please, at the last page of the pamphlet, where the writer refers to 'those who delight in washing the baby's nappies in public'. Would you agree that the word 'nappies' is a bad word?

I don't like it. It's what some call a 'nurseryism'—baby-talk.

Not a word you would expect to find in the serious prose of a sensitive writer?

You might find it in a novel; in the dialogue, I mean.

Would you expect it in a serious political article written by an able, sensitive writer?

No. But literary tastes vary.

The defendant will say that the word revolts him, and he could never have used it. Can you find anything at all in his writings to throw doubt on that statement?

No, unless the pamphlet is part of his writings. And as to that, let me make myself clear. There are pointers in one direction and, I must concede, pointers in the other. The court, I assume, will draw its own conclusions. I have merely been trying to help.

Are you getting a fee for your efforts to help?

I am not.

You say that you have spent many weary hours with the articles. Why were you willing to do that without fee?

I have told you. I wanted to help.

You dislike the defendant's views, you dislike the pamphlet, you thought that the defendant had written the pamphlet, and you wanted to help the plaintiff to recover damages from him?

I don't like that way of putting it.

Which of my propositions is wrong? I'll repeat them—(Counsel does). Can you say that any one of them is wrong?

No. But I must make it plain that the reason why I wanted to help the plaintiff to succeed, was my judgment that the defendant was the author of the pamphlet.

I accept that. But it was a somewhat hasty judgment, would you say?

No. I gave the matter careful thought.

Yet you overlooked some important things? You see that now, don't you?

GEORGE COLMAN, Q.C.

I overlooked some relevant points, I think. How important they
are, is a matter of personal judgment.

*"Tis with our judgments as our watches, none goes just alike, but each
believes his own' Those are the poet's words, aren't they, Professor?*

Ah! Alexander Pope. A wise man.

(The last question is of a type not generally to be commended. But
perhaps, in the special circumstances, it is a permissible and grace-
ful way of rounding off a successful cross-examination and coming
to terms with the witness.)

CHAPTER IX
TIMING

A cross-examiner must decide not only what to do with his witness, but when to do it. In some situations the second question virtually answers itself. In others the order in which topics are introduced or particular questions are put may be of little importance. But more frequently the question of timing deserves serious consideration.

One of the reasons is that the answer to a specific question is so often conditioned by what has gone before. What a witness has already said may coerce him to give a particular answer, or preclude him from saying what he might otherwise have said. An obvious illustration of that is the case where answers which might otherwise have been given are ruled out, from the point of view of the witness, because if he were to give them he would be contradicting himself. But even when that is not so, a witness may feel compelled to refrain from saying something which he is tempted to say because he sees that, in the light of what he has already told the court, the answer will not carry conviction.

Another possibility is that an answer may be influenced by the relationship which has been established between counsel and the witness. The witness may have come to like counsel, or to fear him. He may have been able to infer from what has already happened during his cross-examination, what the cross-examiner would like him to say, or how much information the cross-examiner has on a particular matter.

GEORGE COLMAN, Q.C.

In what follows, an attempt will be made to show how considerations like these should influence counsel's decision about the stage at which he should turn to particular aspects of his inquiry, and about the order in which questions should be put. Reference will be made, also, to certain other factors to which weight should be given by counsel in selecting the most appropriate time sequence in which to put his questions.

An immediate problem which faces counsel when he has heard the evidence in chief (or learnt, at some earlier stage, what the witness would say) is how best to open the cross-examination. A well chosen opening question may take him a long way towards success.

It may be that counsel is lucky enough to have at his command a powerful piece of material, or a strong probability, with which he is able to strike a swift and damaging blow at the structure which the witness is seeking to build up. Even if the point is not a vital one, it is sometimes useful to deliver the blow at once. The impression thus to be made on the court will be helpful to counsel's case; and what is even more important is the effect on the witness. An initial reverse may make him much easier to handle than he would otherwise have been.

Thus, if the circumstances are appropriate, a cross-examination may usefully begin in some such manner as this:

> *You have told the court that at no stage did you see or handle the will. Can you explain how it comes about that your fingerprints appear on three of its pages?*

or:

> *You have convictions for fraud and perjury, have you not?*

or:

> *Why didn't you mention the revolver to the police?*

But counsel, before he takes so bold a line, should satisfy himself that the witness has no escape from the difficulty in which the question is designed to place him. Let us suppose, for example, that the witness asked about the fingerprints on the will is able to say:

> I was in charge of the stationery, and I must have handled the paper at some stage before the will was typed.

In that event counsel has gone about his task clumsily. He has sacrificed necessary caution to drama.

Even when he is not as powerfully equipped as in the examples given, counsel can sometimes devise an opening question which is likely to put the witness in immediate difficulty. A husband, about to be cross-examined in a matrimonial suit about the long history of an unhappy marriage, may not find it easy to answer the following opening question:

> *If you had the whole of your married life to live over again, are there any respects in which you would behave differently?*

If he answers in the negative he is not only claiming an improbable degree of wisdom and virtue; he is giving a reply which is unlikely to stand up to the detailed questions to come. And, some hours later, after it has been shown that on a number of occasions he acted improperly or (at best for him) hastily or unwisely, he may well be faced with this concluding question:

> *Do you still say that if you had your married life to live over again you would behave exactly as you did?*

If, foreseeing something of this sort, the witness responds to the opening question by giving a short list of what he considers to be his errors, he is presenting counsel with a series of openings; and that is something which he probably does not wish to do.

GEORGE COLMAN, Q.C.

But, despite certain misconceptions which are widely entertained, a cross-examination has little in common with a stage drama. If counsel opens in an uninteresting fashion his audience (or at any rate those of them who count) will not start drifting out of the room, whatever their personal inclinations may be. And, more often than not, it is a quiet, cautious opening which is likely to lead to the best results.

Whether counsel has useful material in hand, or whether he is merely hoping to create some as he goes along, he will be wise, often enough, to start off with questions whose main or sole purpose is to give him the measure of his witness. He may be uncertain whether the witness is shrewd or stupid, calm or nervous, candid or deceitful, partisan or unenthusiastic. He may not know whether the witness is educated or uneducated, experienced in some aspect of life or not, or whether he commands or lacks the ability to understand and use language clearly. He may not know whether the witness is a stranger to the litigant who has called him or not; and, if he is a stranger, how his testimony has been obtained. And counsel may wish to find out some of these things, or at any rate to gain impressions about them, before he decides how to go about the important parts of his cross-examination.

To that end, the cross-examiner may find it best to begin by asking questions about the witness himself, or about some matter which is no more than marginally relevant to the inquiry. He will be seeking replies which, even though they may have little bearing upon the case, will teach him something about the witness.

In many instances counsel will think it important to establish a friendly relationship with the witness, or to build up his confidence. And, for that purpose, he may find it appropriate to start with a series of questions whose answers are predictable, and not controversial. Thus:

I think there are certain things about which we shall agree, Mr. Grey. It is never easy to guess how the Stock Exchange is going to behave, is it?

No, it's not easy. But there are certain signs which we have learnt
to recognize.

Yes. And in this case some of the familiar signs were present, were they?

Yes.

*One of them, I take it, was the current talk about devaluation of the
pound. Is that so?*

That was, to my mind, a significant pointer.

Would that sort of talk tend to inflate the price of gold shares?

It always does; but there are dangers attached to that.

What are they?

What usually happens is that, for one reason or another, the
rumour is dispelled, and down come the gold shares.

Were you, then, pessimistic about gold shares?

I'm supposed to be pessimistic about the market generally. I prefer to call myself cautious.

*If I may suggest it, any approach to the future of the share market calls for
caution. Would you agree?*

Readily.

*And any prediction you may make is, in a sense, tentative. It is subject to
a number of reservations, is it not?*

Yes.

If the witness is a young child, much may depend upon the
extent to which counsel is able to win his or her confidence. This,
if it can be achieved at all, will be achieved by asking in a quiet,
friendly manner, a series of simple questions which the child will
enjoy answering. Normally, the court will be patient with a cross-
examiner who, within reasonable limits, takes up time in this way:

Do you go to school, Mary?

Yes.

Who is your teacher?

Miss Green.

Do you like her?

Yes, but she sometimes gets cross.

Did you tell her about the motor accident?

No. She didn't ask me.

Will you tell me some things about it, please?

Daddy was driving along our road and the lorry hit us. I was bleeding like anything.

Was it very sore?

Not so very.

Did you cry?

A little bit. Not so very much.

Are you a brave girl?

Yes. My mother said I was. And so did John.

Now I'm going to ask you about the lorry. Will you listen carefully to what I ask, Mary?

With such a witness, counsel may be called upon to exercise great patience throughout the cross-examination.

Patience, indeed, is an essential quality in a cross-examiner. If, for example, counsel's aim is to reveal the untruthfulness or unreliability of his opponent's witnesses by bringing out conflicts between them on points of detail, it may be his duty, at the risk of boring himself and the court, to spend a good deal of time inquiring into details which are of no great importance in themselves. And the process may have to be repeated with witness after witness. The easiest method of doing this is to take the events in chronological order. But, particularly when it is thought that the witnesses are being deliberately untruthful, another method is sometimes preferable. A fabricated story is usually invented and memorized in chronological order, and discrepancies are more likely to appear if that order is departed from in cross-examination. Counsel may dart back and forth, at random, among the details of the story, and that may help him to achieve his object. But it will be better still if he can build bridges across which to lead his witness from one part of the narrative to another. What is meant by that metaphor will appear from the following example:

In what counsel thinks may be a fabricated account, a mother has described how, on a winter's afternoon, she and her daughter walked together, for about a mile, to a doctor's house. Asked about the weather, she has said that it was raining quite heavily during the walk. Now the daughter is testifying. Counsel could ask her, as he did her mother, about the state of the weather during the walk, and then go on to deal with what happened at the doctor's house. He prefers to start with their arrival at the house, and build a bridge back to the question whether it had been raining:

Into what room were you shown at the doctor's house?
A waiting-room.
Was that a large, attractively-furnished room with a fire burning in it?
Yes.
What was the first thing that you and your mother did when you got into that room?
We sat down on a couch.
The couch is under the window, isn't it?
Yes, I think so.
You didn't, either of you, go and stand by the fire?
No, I wasn't cold. We'd had a brisk walk.
Physically, were you quite comfortable?
Yes, as far as I remember.
Did you keep your coats on in that room?
My mother did. I took mine off and held it on my lap.
Inside out?
No.
It didn't make your skirt wet?
No. The coat was quite dry.
If your shoes and stockings had been wet would you have gone to the fire?
I suppose so. But I don't think they were.
So it didn't rain during your walk?
No.

Another matter which governs the order in which counsel will put his questions is the one which has already been referred to as 'closing the escape routes'. This, too, relates to dishonest

GEORGE COLMAN, Q.C.

witnesses. When counsel has a question to put to a witness which ought to evoke a helpful answer, it is important to consider the likelihood that the witness will, if possible, lie his way out of giving that answer. Counsel, before he puts the important question, will consider the lies which the witness may resort to, and try to make it impossible for the witness to make use of them. Here is a simple illustration:

Some important papers have been taken by a burglar from the study of a scientist's house, and the witness, who has connections with a foreign government, is suspected of having taken them. He was seen walking away from the front door of the house, but says that he was never inside it. He had been to the front door to inquire where the nearest police station was, but had had no response to his knocking:

> *Did you know that this was Dr. Maroon's house?*
> I did not.
> *Did you think it was the house of someone you knew?*
> No.
> *But how could you go knocking at the door of a stranger's house at that hour of the night?*
> I had to find a police station urgently. And I knew I wouldn't be pulling people out of their beds. I chose that house because I saw through the curtains that there were lights on in it.
> *Where were the lights?*
> In the kitchen and in one of the rooms upstairs.

The witness appears to have made a slip. The obvious question is how he knew which was the kitchen if the windows were curtained, and he had never been inside the house. But if the question is put at once, the witness may take one of the many escape routes which are open to him. Counsel seeks to close them in this fashion:

> *Did you make any effort to see if there were people moving about in the house?*

CROSS-EXAMINATION

No. I couldn't see through the curtains.

If you go close enough you can sometimes peep through a chink in the curtains.

I didn't see any chinks, and I didn't go close. I'm not the sort of person who goes prowling about peeping through other people's windows.

Did you go straight to the front door?

Yes. And straight away from it when no one answered.

Had you never visited Dr. Maroon?

I'd never heard of Dr. Maroon.

Had you ever visited anyone in that house?

Never.

You did not set foot in that house on that night or on any other occasion?

No. Or in that street. I don't think I was within a mile of it in my life.

Was there smoke coming from any of the chimneys?

I didn't notice. You don't seem to understand. I wasn't a burglar casing a joint. I was an honest citizen trying to make a simple inquiry.

Had anyone ever told you about that house?

What about that house?

Anything about that house?

No. I don't move in those circles.

Which circles?

Scientific circles; I understand this Dr. Maroon is a scientist.

Perhaps before he moved into it?

I thought I'd made myself plain. I had never heard of Maroon or any of his friends or relations or landlords or predecessors or any of their houses or safes or secrets or papers.

Then how did you know which was the kitchen?

It is the sad fate of many a brave effort like this one that one escape route has been overlooked, and that the witness skips gaily down it. The answer may be:

GEORGE COLMAN, Q.C.

> Well, I'd be surprised if they kept their garbage can just outside a door leading into their living-room.

Or it may be:

> I happen to be an architect. Twenty years ago I designed a standard house for a speculative builder. He built fifty of them, all over the town. And I could see at a glance that this was one of them.

One of the difficulties about closing escape routes is this: An astute liar may see what counsel is about, and adjust his answers so as to leave one of the routes open. When there seems to be a danger of that, counsel will not set about closing the escape routes as soon as he sees his opening. He will, at that stage, start cross-examining about some other aspect of the case, and introduce the necessary questions later on, when the witness is less likely to remember the answer which suggested the line of inquiry to counsel. If possible, the blocking questions will not be asked one after the other, but will be scattered among other material. And each will be introduced in a context designed to mask its relevance.

Thus, in the case with which the previous example dealt, counsel might think it safer, as soon as the kitchen is mentioned, to start asking questions about the connection between the witness and the foreign power. He might ask (even if there is no reason to expect an affirmative answer) whether the witness was not, while in a foreign country, told about Dr. Maroon and his work. A denial can then be followed, plausibly, by the question whether, then, the witness had never heard of Dr. Maroon:

> Never.
>
> *Did they or anyone else never mention a scientist who lived in that street or that area?*
>
> No.
>
> *Did they then, or anyone at any time, tell you anything about the experiments which were being conducted in that area?*

CROSS-EXAMINATION

No.

Or about any house in that area?

No.

Counsel might then spend some time on the need of the witness to find a police station, and then ask him whether he had no idea where to find one:

Not the slightest.

Why didn't you use a public telephone?

I hadn't the faintest idea where to find one.

Had you never been in the area?

Never in my life.

Similarly, the other necessary questions will be introduced when the mind of the witness has been focused on something remote from his reference to the kitchen.

When the witness has said something which is in conflict with what one of counsel's own witnesses will say later in the case, the conflicting version must be put to the witness. But it is not always advisable to put it as soon as the statement is made. If that is done, the witness may at once correct or modify his answer and suffer less damage to his credibility than he will suffer if counsel first attempts to pin down firmly the erroneous statement which he has made.

A business man, let us suppose, has said that a variation of a contract between his firm and a company in Italy was orally agreed upon when he had lunch with the chairman of the Italian company in London on a particular day. He gives a plausible explanation for the fact that the variation was never put into writing, and says that the Italian witness will be testifying untruthfully if he denies that the agreement was made, or that he lunched with the witness. It so happens that the restaurant at which the event is alleged to have taken place was not open on the day referred to by the witness, and counsel is able to prove that. He should not be precipitate in putting that fact to the witness. If, prematurely, he says:

163

GEORGE COLMAN, Q.C.

> *I shall be calling evidence to prove that Bianchi's Restaurant was closed on the 11th of June. How, then, can you say that you and Signor Rosso lunched there?*

the witness may say:

Oh, did I say the 11th? I meant the 9th.

or

> I beg your pardon. That was a slip of my tongue. I meant the other Italian Restaurant, Bardolini's.

Counsel might be more fortunate (though he might not) if he were to keep back his important piece of information until after something of this sort:

> *How, after all this time, can you be so sure of the date?*
> I have the lunch appointment noted in a pocket diary. Here it is, if you care to look at it.
> *Thank you. ... The entry seems to have been squeezed in between two others. Why is that?*
> That is because I wasn't expecting to make a lunch appointment, and I didn't leave space for one. I fitted the note in when Signor Rosso telephoned me at about noon.
> *Who chose the restaurant?*
> I did. It's the place to which I always take visiting Italians. If you're interested, they give you a very good meal there.
> *Do they? What did you eat that day? Do you remember?*
> Yes. I had an excellent arrosto di vitello. And I can tell you what Signor Rosso had, too, if you like?
> *Yes, what was it?*
> Ossobuco.
> *Where, in the restaurant, did you sit?*
> In the alcove, underneath the picture of St. Peter's.
> *And, I take it, you shared a bottle of Italian wine. ... What are you laughing at?*

CROSS-EXAMINATION

I'm laughing because Signor Rosso said his favourite wine was whisky and soda. And that is what we had.

Signor Rosso tells me that he did say that to you, but it was in Milan, a year or so earlier. And that he never lunched with you in London.

He is lying. I remember vividly his remarking that he'd never had a better ossobuco even in his own country.

So you are certain of the date, you are certain you lunched together at Bianchi's, you know exactly where you sat, and what you had to eat, and you remember clearly two things which were said on that day and in that place?

I've told you so.

You have no doubt on any of these points?

Not one iota of a doubt.

I shall prove that on the night of the 10th of June there was a fire at Bianchi's, as a result of which the restaurant was closed on the 11th and 12th of June. What do you say to that?

A comment may be interpolated here upon the form of the long question in which counsel summarized several points in the evidence which the witness had given. It was not essential to do that; but it is sometimes useful to frame such questions in order to emphasize what has been said. With a jury, particularly, such emphasis may be useful, and it is not uncommon for competent counsel to end a cross-examination with a summarized reiteration of that kind, or of a slightly different kind. Thus:

So you have told the court that your overdraft had been called up by the bank?

Yes.

And that your efforts to borrow money elsewhere had failed?

Yes.

That you were having difficulty with your plant?

Yes.

And that the regular purchaser of half your output had cancelled his contract with you?

GEORGE COLMAN, Q.C.

Yes.

And you still *say that you had reasonable prospects of meeting your financial obligations?*

A problem of timing which is not always easy to resolve arises when a witness has given an answer (perhaps on a minor point) which conflicts with what he has said in his evidence in chief, or earlier in his cross-examination. If there is any possibility of a reconciliation or explanation, counsel should draw the attention of the witness to the conflict; and even if there is no such possibility, he may wish to do so in order to bring the shortcomings of the witness to the notice of the court at an early stage. These things can, of course, be done in argument. But if the point is left until that stage, it may lose some of its force.

Among the many other things which a cross-examiner has to consider is the psychology of his tribunal. And not least important, under this heading, is the reluctance of human beings to change their minds. A court which has to resolve a dispute of fact will, however hard it tries to keep an open mind, be forming provisional views about the witnesses while the evidence is being given. And once a strong view of that kind has taken root, it may be difficult to displace. It is for that reason, mainly, that experienced counsel sometimes decide to ask questions of the type which has been illustrated, which do no more than summarize or emphasize what is already on the record. Another reason which sometimes operates is counsel's desire to jolt the witness into a realization of what he has said; in some situations and with some witnesses, the realization may have a salutary effect upon the manner in which the witness will respond to further questions.

These considerations may play a part, too, when the witness has given two conflicting answers, and counsel has to decide whether to face him with the conflict as soon as it arises, or to defer that process. His decision may depend upon the manner in which the answers to these problems present themselves to him.

Has the court probably noticed the conflict?

CROSS-EXAMINATION

If not, is it desirable to point it out at once so that they will realize at this stage that the witness is not as reliable as they may think?

Is it likely to help me in my further cross-examination if the witness is made to see his blunder?

Or am I likely to do better with him if I don't put him on his guard by bringing the conflict to his notice at this stage?

The consideration raised in the last of these questions may be a decisive one. There is many a witness who, having made a bad impression throughout his evidence, leaves the courtroom feeling that he has done very well. Such a witness might do better if he had the benefit, during his cross-examination, of having his mistakes and deficiencies pointed out to him as they arose.

It is on similar principles that counsel may decide whether or not to reveal the extent of his own information about some matter touching the testimony of the witness. It is one of his great advantages that the witness, very often, does not know how much his cross-examiner really knows or understands about something; and that lack of knowledge is a considerable handicap to one who is inclined to lie. Here, again, counsel will have to decide, in the light of all the circumstances, whether to put a question, at an early stage, which will indicate to the witness that he (counsel) knows a good deal about something, and so put fetters upon a tendency to lie. The alternative is to frame questions in such a manner that the witness, believing that counsel is uninformed, will talk himself into an untenable position.

Lastly, on the subject of timing, a reference must be made to the effect which adjournments may have upon the success of a cross-examination. It is seldom that a case of any importance, which involves conflicts of fact, can be concluded during a single sitting of the court. Consequently, a witness who is under cross-examination often has the opportunity, overnight, over a weekend, or during some longer or shorter interval, of speaking to others, including people who have been or will be witnesses on the

GEORGE COLMAN, Q.C.

same side. If such a break comes at an inappropriate time, from counsel's point of view, a promising line of cross-examination may be frustrated.

It may seem to a reader of this book that counsel has been enjoined to keep his attention on so many things that he is expected to be the intellectual counterpart of a juggler who keeps a football, half a dozen cups and saucers, a top hat and an umbrella in the air at once. Perhaps he is. And now it must be added that, for the reason which has been indicated, he should keep his eye on the clock.

If there is a question, or series of questions, which should be asked before the witness has time to speak to others, counsel should be careful to leave himself enough time to do this before the court adjourns. And to that end he may find it necessary to break off in the middle of some other topic. This sort of thing is quite common:

We'll come back to that part of the case tomorrow morning, Mr. White. Now, before the court adjourns, tell me about something else. Did you get any information about the dog from Miss Amber?

I can't remember any.

I want you to think very hard please. If you have any recollection at all of any talk between yourself and Miss Amber about the dog, I want the court to hear about it now. Have you any?

No, I haven't.

Can I take it that if she had told you anything about the dog, you would remember it?

Yes, I think so.

Surely you can be more positive than that. Could you have forgotten such a conversation?

No.

An alternative course which can effectively be followed by counsel who is sure that he is on strong ground, is to invite the witness to make full use of the coming adjournment:

CROSS-EXAMINATION

I'm going to put a question to you, Mr. Green, which you need not answer now; think about it overnight, and tell the court tomorrow morning: If you were satisfied that you had a valid lease, how did you come to write the letter Exhibit 'J'?

If, on the following morning, the witness can give no acceptable explanation, his failure to do so will perhaps seem more significant than if he had not had time for reflection.

CHAPTER X
PRIVATE EYE

In the foregoing chapters a number of the techniques of cross-examination have been discussed and illustrated. In most of the illustrations the witnesses have fared ill, and the cross-examiners have been dramatically successful.

In contrast to those, the reader is now to be presented with something a little closer to the real life of the courts. The witness is untruthful, but it is not possible for counsel to demonstrate that conclusively. What he can do, however, is to demonstrate the probability that the witness is lying—to reveal to the court the fact that the man testifying is one upon whom it would be dangerous to rely.

That is as much as a cross-examiner can hope to achieve in the ordinary course of events. But it is no insignificant achievement. If his own witnesses fare better, he will probably win his case. That his client, gratified by the outcome, will be wholly unconscious of the skill and good judgment which counsel has exercised in achieving it is perhaps unfortunate: but it is normal.

What follows is part of an imaginary cross-examination of a private detective. The sentences in bold type represent the unspoken thoughts of the cross-examiner.

The detective has been called on behalf of a brewer who alleges that the defendant, the owner of a public house, has, in breach of a contract between them, been promoting the sale of a rival beer at the expense of the plaintiff's product, and, furthermore, making damaging statements or insinuations about the plaintiff's beer. The

CROSS-EXAMINATION

plaintiff's beer is called Red Seal and the rival beer Blank's Ale. The defendant is alleged to have acted through two barmen employed by him, but counsel has been instructed that both of them will deny that they ever did anything of the kind alleged against them.

The private detective's evidence in chief is that he visited the defendant's bar on a number of occasions during the week ending Saturday, 4th June, in order to watch the barmen and listen to their conversations with customers. On one of those occasions he was accompanied by his wife. Twice, when he inquired about Red Seal beer, he was told by one of the barmen that he (the barman) could not recommend it and was advised to try Blank's Ale. On five occasions he heard other customers being told that Red Seal was unpopular or unsatisfactory and advised to take Blank's instead. The dates and times were specified. On Saturday, 4th June, at about 1 p.m. a man entered the bar, had a whispered conversation with the barman and was shown some figures. The man then handed the barman a few banknotes, and left. The witness followed this man, and saw him enter the offices of the defendant. The cross-examination begins:

(This seedy-looking character is going to stick to his story. He's got it well prepared, I'm sure. But I've got one jolt for him, at least. Shall I open up with it, so as to soften him up a bit? No; I'll find out more about him first. Let's begin at the beginning.)

When, where, and by whom were you asked to make this investigation?
By Mr. White, sir, the plaintiff's sales manager. I went to his office on the 27th of May last year.
You seem to be taking the date from some document. What is it?
It's a letter, sir, which I wrote confirming our engagement.
Let me see it, phase.... Thank you.... I see that you call yourselves The Steelgrey and Black Private Investigation Bureau?
Yes, sir.
You are Mr. Black. Who is Steelgrey?
Steelgrey is my wife's maiden name.

171

GEORGE COLMAN, Q.C.

Is she a member of the firm?
As I've indicated, sir, she assists me at times.
Was she assisting you before you married her?
No, sir. I married her long before I started this business.
Then what is her maiden name doing on your letterhead?
I just thought it would sound better.
You wanted to make your firm look more impressive than it really is?
You can put it that way, sir. It's a normal business device.

(So that's the type he is: I wonder if the reference to Scotland Yard is a bluff, too. They don't seem to know about him. I'll try my luck.)

And is it a normal business device to describe yourself on your letterhead as 'formerly of Scotland Yard'?
I don't know what you mean, sir. I *was* at Scotland Yard.

(If he says so, I suppose it's true. But I'd better go through with it.)

When?
In 1961, sir, and a bit of 1962.
For a little over a year, at most?
Just under a year, actually.
Why did you leave Scotland Yard?
Of my own account, sir. To better myself.
Who was your immediate superior at Scotland Yard?
Mr. Scarlet.
What was his rank?
He didn't actually have a rank, sir. He was just called Mr. Scarlet. We weren't on the police side.
What side were you on?
We were in the filing office.
So you were a filing clerk at Scotland Yard?
Yes, but I learnt a lot about police methods. I used to study the documents.

CROSS-EXAMINATION

Did you consider it honest to advertise yourself to the public as ' formerly of Scotland Yard' when you had been no more than a filing clerk there?
It wasn't a lie, sir.

(Enough of that. But here's something else on the letterhead before I get to the letter itself.)

You say 'assisted by a staff of trained investigators'. Who are they?
Well, there's my wife, and Miss Lemon.
Is that all?
At the time of this investigation we had a Mr. Brown working for us.

(That must be the man the barman saw with him.)

Did Miss Lemon and Mr. Brown take any part in this investigation?
No, sir. ... Not Miss Lemon. Mr. Brown did a bit of work, I think, but it led to nothing.
He was with you in the bar once, wasn't he?
Yes. For half an hour or so, but he didn't hear anything, as far as I remember.

(He's being vague about this. Why isn't he sure about what Brown heard or didn't hear? I'd better find out more about Brown.)

Where is Mr. Brown now?
He's not with us any longer.
I gathered that from your previous answer. The question was: Where is he now?
I don't really know, sir.
You don't seem quite sure about what he heard, if anything. Didn't he tell you at the time?
He must have, but it couldn't have been helpful, sir, because there's nothing about it in my notes made at the time.

GEORGE COLMAN, Q.C.

(So he made notes. I'll come back to that later.)

Can't you remember?
I remember that his evidence was disappointing. I can't remember the exact details.
But you do remember clearly that he did some work on the investigation, do you?
Oh, yes, sir.
Then why did you say, when I first asked you about it, that you thought *he had done a bit of work on the investigation?*
Is that what I said? It was a slip, sir.
I gather that you haven't a very good memory?
You're wrong, sir. I have a good memory for what is important. But I don't remember unimportant things.
Well, perhaps what Mr. Brown heard or did not hear is more important to my client than to yours. Have you no idea at all where he is?
No, it wouldn't help your client, sir. It's just that he couldn't hear clearly because of the noise in the bar.
Your memory seems to be improving a little. But I asked you whether you had no idea at all where Brown is now. Will you answer that question?
I can't honestly say I know where he is.

(He is trying to hide something. It's worth pressing.)

Come, Mr. Black. Have you no idea at all where he can be found?
Well, he's in prison somewhere, but I honestly don't know where.
In prison, is he? For what?
Perjury, sir.
In relation to one of your firm's investigations?
Yes. I foolishly left him to do one without supervision. I had nothing to do with it. Naturally, I sacked him as soon as I knew.

(This letterhead is a gift. Let me see if I can squeeze a little more out of it.)

CROSS-EXAMINATION

Where was your 'staff of trained investigators' trained, and by whom?
I trained them myself, sir.
Oh, did you? And who trained you?
(After a pause)—I'd prefer not to say.
I'm afraid you must.
I was trained by the Federal Bureau of Investigation. You know, in the United States, sir.

(That doesn't sound true. Let's see.)

When were you there?
For most of 1963. Actually February to November.
What were you there, a filing clerk?
No, sir. I was on the criminal investigation staff.
Why didn't you put that on your letterhead?
I didn't think the F.B.I. would like it. It's a very confidential organization.
Did they ever indicate that you were to keep it secret?
Not in so many words. But I thought I'd better not risk annoying them. You see, I'm intending to rejoin them. I only came back to England because my mother was dying.

(He got in ahead of me with that one. But he's not out of the wood yet.)

Who was your superior officer at the F.B.I.?
That I can't tell you, sir. It's confidential.
Where, exactly, were you trained?
I'm afraid that's also confidential.
Am I right in supposing that you'll give that answer to anything I ask you about your association with the F.B.I.?
I'm afraid so, sir. You see, I took an oath of secrecy.

(How can I get round that? I'll go back a bit.)

GEORGE COLMAN, Q.C.

How did you come to join the F.B.I.?

A firm here sent me to the States on a mission. I had to work with the F.B.I. on that, and then I decided to join them.

The name of the firm and the nature of the mission are confidential, I suppose?

Yes, sir. Please don't press me to talk about it.

(The court won't like it if I do. But I wonder if he really was in the United States.)

Did you go to the United States by sea or by air?

By sea, sir.

On what date?

January or February. I'm not sure of the exact date.

And did you return by sea?

Yes, in November; I left on about the 24th.

I want the exact dates. Will you be good enough to bring your passport to court tomorrow?

It won't show on my passport, sir.

Why not?

My mission was a secret one, so I travelled under a false name, on a false passport.

Whose passport?

No one's. It was a forged passport which a friend in the passport office got for me.

So you committed a fraud on the immigration authorities in this country and the United States?

Well, you can call it that, sir. But in my business we have to do these things.

Where is the forged passport?

I've destroyed it, sir.

Under what name did you travel?

That's very confidential. It could have terrible consequences for my client at that time if I gave you the name.

On what ship did you go to America?... You are hesitating. That isn't confidential. What ship, please?

CROSS-EXAMINATION

(He doesn't want to commit himself.)

I think it was the *Queen Mary*. I may be mistaken.
On what ship did you return?
I think it was the same ship.

(I don't think he knows the names of any other ships which go to the U.S.A.)

How many times have you been to the United States?
Only that once, sir.
And you can't remember the name of the ship you travelled on?
I think it was the *Queen Mary*. I'm almost certain. It was some years ago.
And you think it was the same ship that brought you home again. You're not even sure of that?
I'm almost sure. It was a long time ago.
But you remember that it was at 1.57 p.m. that you heard a barman say something on the 3rd of June last year?
But that was in my notes, sir. I went through them just before giving my evidence.
But you have a good memory for what is important, you say. Were those things in your notes not important?
The words were. Not the exact times, I think.

(That's fair enough. But did he make the notes under the barmen's noses?)

Would your memory not retain minor details like the times?
No. Especially as there were so many of them.
Would you be able to remember the times now?
I don't think so, sir.
Although you studied your notes less than an hour ago?
No, sir.
For how long could you remember details of that sort?

177

GEORGE COLMAN, Q.C.

I really don't know, sir.

Well, we can try a little test, here in court. Do you think you'll be able to remember some figures if I give them to you now and ask for them in fifteen minutes' time?

I think so, sir. But I won't guarantee it.

When did you make the notes which you looked through this morning?

They were typed out by my wife in the office each day when I got back there.

You dictated them to her?

Yes, except for her own statement about the day she was with me in the bar.

You dictated the times and all the details from memory?

No, sir. I had my rough notes, which I'd made in the bar about some of the details.

You made notes in the bar on each visit?

Yes.

So the barmen could easily have noticed that you were writing down what they said, could they?

I tried to do it when they weren't looking.

But there were two of them. And you were in the bar on several occasions. Surely you were taking a considerable risk that they'd suspect you. People don't usually stand at a bar counter making notes, do they?

I did it very unobtrusively, sir.

How do you take notes unobtrusively at a bar counter?

On the margin of my newspaper, sir. I had it open at the crossword puzzle.

(That's cunning.... Oh, well. You can't expect to hit a bullseye every time.)

Will you produce the newspaper, please?

There were a few newspapers, sir, but I can't produce them. They've been destroyed.

Who destroyed them?

I did. They only had rough jottings on them. And all that, with what I remembered directly, was put in the typed notes.

CROSS-EXAMINATION

Didn't they teach you at the F.B.I. that it's important to keep your original notes?

No, sir. On the contrary.

(That's an odd one.)

'On the contrary.' Will you be good enough to explain what you mean by that?

I was taught that if the matter may go to court it's wiser to destroy your original notes as soon as you've transferred them to a fair copy.*

Did they really tell you that?

Yes, sir.

Did they give you any reason?

They said that once counsel gets hold of the original notes he's almost bound to find something which will make trouble for you in cross-examination.

(I want to see those notes. I'd better get him to use them.)

What was the exact time, on the Tuesday, when the tall barman spoke to the man he called Bill?

Do you want me to try to remember without my notes? I'm afraid I can't. I'm on oath, you know.

You may look at your notes.

It was 9.17 p.m., sir.

Thank you. Now hand me those notes, please. ... We'll come to them later. I want to go back to your letter to your client. You quote a fee there for the investigation.

If I may say so, sir, I wasn't quoting a fee. I was confirming an agreement.

Quite so. And part of the agreement you confirm in these terms: 'Should our inquiries produce satisfactory results we are to receive a bonus of £200 in addition to these fees.'

---

* *AUTHOR'S NOTE:* No letters of demand from the F.B.I. please. This witness is a liar.

GEORGE COLMAN, Q.C.

Is that your normal type of arrangement?

Oh, yes, sir. I've had legal advice. There's nothing improper about it.

What did you mean by satisfactory results? Success in this case?

Not at all. That would have been improper. I meant if we heard the barmen saying the sort of thing our client believed they were saying.

What would have been improper about the other type of arrangement?

That would have affected my impartiality, sir. I mean it might have looked like that.

How does it look now? I don't understand, sir.

Have you had your money yet?

No, sir.

And if the court finds that your evidence is a pack of lies, do you expect to get it?

No. But I wouldn't perjure myself for a paltry £200, sir, really I wouldn't.

For how much would you perjure yourself?

For no amount on earth, sir.

Not even in filling out a United States immigration form?

I don't think that was on oath. Here I'm on oath.

By the way, when did you say you left the United States?

About the 25th of November, 1963.

What were people talking about during your last few days there?

Talking about, sir? Which people?

Can you remember anything of interest in the newspapers at that time?

I'm not much of a newspaper reader, sir. ... Do you mean the assassination of President Kennedy perhaps?

(Perhaps he was there. But not at the F.B.I. I think. But why is he evasive about the ship? I must see if I can get anything out of his wife on that when she gives evidence.)

Yes, that's what I meant. Now let me look at your notes. ... I see that you were in the bar on the Monday, twice, and on the Tuesday with your

CROSS-EXAMINATION

wife; then on the Friday and Saturday. Why not on the Wednesday and Thursday?

I didn't want to make myself too conspicuous. So I gave it a rest for a couple of days. In the meanwhile I changed my appearance.

How did you do that?

I'd been wearing long hair. I had it cut short. I dyed my eyebrows and eyelashes. I put on a pair of black-rimmed glasses. And I went there in an open-necked shirt on the Friday and Saturday.

(So that's why they say they didn't see him after Tuesday. Now I'd better get on to the question of his hearing. If he says the barmen spoke loudly, it will be improbable. If he says softly, how did he manage to hear so clearly?)

Where were you standing on the Tuesday evening?

I wasn't standing, sir. We sat on stools just to the left of the cash register. My wife was with me.

(So she was. I'd almost forgotten. There's something else I must deal with before I ask him how he heard. And at the same time I'll prepare the ground about his trip to America.)

Have you discussed this matter with your wife?

(He won't be foolish enough to say he hasn't, surely.)

Oh, yes, sir.

When?

During the last couple of days; and, of course, when we made the notes.

By the way, how long have you been married to her?

Ten years, approximately.

Did she go to the United States with you?

No, sir.

Did she see you off on the ship?... Well, did she?

181

GEORGE COLMAN, Q.C.

I'm just trying to remember, sir.

What are you looking for at the back of the court? Your wife isn't in here. Oh, I see; the clock. Why this sudden interest in the time?

I was just wondering about the time, sir. There's no special reason.

If you are wondering whether your wife will be giving evidence before you have a chance to talk to her, I'll try to help you. She may well be; but I can't be sure.

It wasn't that at all, sir.

Well, answer my question, please.

What was the question, sir?

Don't you know? Have you really forgotten the question?

About the ship, sir?

Yes. Did she see you off?

No, sir. I don't think so, sir.

Did she meet you at the docks on your return?

No. ... I don't think so.

Does she know the names of the ship or ships?

I don't know, sir.

Does she know what you were doing in America?

No, sir. It was confidential.

Does she not even know that you were with the F.B.I.?

I was told to keep it secret.

You have told the court that you are planning to rejoin the F.B.I. Have you not even told your wife about that?

(He doesn't like that one. Unless he can get to her before she is asked, she's going to say he didn't tell her. But he sees how improbable it is that he should have told her nothing.)

Well?

No, sir.

Not even that you hoped to go to some job in America?

Well, you see, sir, it's like this. She's very fond of this country, and it might upset our marriage if I started to talk about leaving it.

CROSS-EXAMINATION

(I'd better get back to the merits if I'm to have a chance of cross-examining her before the next adjournment.)

> *When you and your wife discussed the matter on the Tuesday evening, did your recollection coincide with hers?*

Yes, sir.

In every detail?

On every point of any importance.

I gather from that that there were points on which your recollection differed. Am I right?

There may have been one or two trifles. I won't be able to remember them, I'm afraid.

Can I take it that you were in complete agreement about what the barman said?

Yes, sir. We were very careful about that.

Did she remember precisely what you remembered about that?

She did, sir.

She was able to confirm every word of the conversation?

Yes, sir.

(That's not very likely. I hope the court sees that.)

> *On which side of you did your wife sit?*

On my left-hand side.

Where was the man whom the barman called Bill?

About two yards to my right, sir.

Those points you have discussed with your wife, have you?

Yes, sir.

Was Bill standing, or sitting on a stool?

Standing, I think. I'm not quite sure.

The bar was crowded, was it not?

Fairly crowded. ... Doesn't my note say that?

Your note says very crowded.

Then that would be right, sir.

GEORGE COLMAN, Q.C.

Was there no one between you and Bill?

A group of three men, sir.

I take it, then, that they were even better placed than you were to hear what was said?

From their position, sir, yes. But I was listening. They were talking and laughing among themselves.

Were they the only people in the bar who were talking and laughing?

Others were talking, too.

Tell the court again about the conversation between the barman and Bill, please?

The gentleman said: 'I think I'll try this new Red Seal stuff', and the barman answered: 'Sure, Bill, if you want to poison yourself. But take my advice and stick to Blank's.' The gentleman said: 'Well, you should know; give me a Blank's.'

Did the barman say that in a loud, clear voice?

No, sir. He leant over and said it quietly.

In a whisper?

No. In a quiet conversational tone.

And how is it that in that rather noisy bar you were able to hear so clearly what was said in a quiet, conversational tone?

My hearing is exceptionally good, sir.

(We'll soon see if that is so. I'll put my next couple of questions very quietly.)

(In a very quiet voice)—*Now who could have told you that?*

Many people have told me that, sir.

(Spoken so softly that it is almost inaudible, and with counsel's face turned away from the witness)—*Do you consider yourself unique in that regard?*

(Promptly)—I won't say unique, sir, but I've never met anyone whose hearing was anything like as good as mine.

(His hearing is remarkably good. I'll be surprised if his wife does as well when I test her.)

CROSS-EXAMINATION

What was Mr. Brown's hearing like?

Just about average, I'd say, sir. That's why, on the Monday, he failed to hear what I heard.

Were the words on the Monday spoken in the same confidential tone?

Yes, sir. The tall barman always used that tone. The other one spoke a bit louder, but, as I've told you, all he ever said was 'We don't stock it; people don't seem to like it; try a Blank's'.

Was the noise in the bar any more or less when Brown was there than on any other occasion?

It was just about the same at all times, sir.

Had you told your client that you had abnormally acute hearing?

Mr. White, sir? He mentioned it to me, sir. He said he'd heard that I had that gift and that's why he'd approached me. Apparently some of his staff had tried to get the evidence, but couldn't hear.

So he found the right man, it seems?

If I may say so, sir, I don't think anyone else could have done this job.

You mean no one without your abnormally acute hearing?

That's what I mean, sir.

(His ears are sharper than his wits.)

Well, if that is so, how is it that your wife, who lacks your gift, and who was a little further away than you, was able to hear everything that you heard?

Oh, her hearing is very good too—almost as good as mine.

Almost as good as yours, did you say? Will she stand up to the test I gave you a little while ago?

Unfortunately she's got a bit of a cold today, sir, and that affects her hearing. But normally she's pretty nearly as good as I am. That's my opinion anyhow. Others may disagree.

I thought you expressed a different opinion a little while ago. Did you not?

I, sir? No. You must have misunderstood me.

GEORGE COLMAN, Q.C.

Did you not say that you had never met anyone whose hearing was anything approaching yours in acuteness?
I don't think those were my words, sir.
I have someone with me who made a note of your words. Let me read them to you:
'I've never met anyone whose hearing was anything like as good as mine.'
Did you say that?
I'm afraid I was being a little boastful. I'd like to apologize, sir, for the words 'anything like'.
Did those words represent your honest belief or not?
Well, not really, sir.

(I think I'll hammer it home a little.)

So you lied to the court?
If you put it like that.
I do put it like that. And when you said that you didn't think that anyone without your abnormally acute hearing could have done this job, was that a lie, too?
It wasn't a statement of fact, sir. It was just a point of view I was expressing.
Yes, but was it a point of view which you truly held?
I'm a bit confused now, sir. Would you please clarify your question?
I'll put my difficulty to you in a different way. Your wife heard every word, you tell me. Was that true, or would you like to correct it?
(Sadly)—It was true, sir.
But her hearing was not as good as yours. Or do you now say it was?
It was good.
Was it as good as yours?
No, sir.
So it is not correct that the job couldn't have been done by anyone without your abnormally acute hearing, is it?
It was safer with me, sir.
Will you please answer my question? Was the statement I put to you correct?
Not quite.

CROSS-EXAMINATION

And you knew that when you made the statement, did you not?

I'm finding it a bit hard to concentrate, sir.

(He's very unhappy. Now is the time to talk about the Saturday incident.)

At about one o'clock on the Saturday a man came and spoke to the shorter barman, you say?

Yes, sir.

From where did you take your time?

From my watch, sir. I check it with the wireless every day.

What was the exact time?

When I said about one o'clock in my notes I meant within a minute, one way or the other, of that time.

You didn't hear what was said?

They were whispering, sir.

With your excellent hearing could you not pick up a word of what they said?

When the barman was showing him that paper with the figures on it I thought I heard the word 'pints' used. It was difficult to be sure.

Why did you not say that in your evidence in chief? Or in your notes?

Because I wasn't sure, sir. I wanted to be very careful.

But the word 'pints' fits into the picture, doesn't it?

I don't understand, sir.

What did you think the money was paid to the barman for?

I had an open mind on that at the time.

And when you saw the man enter the defendant's office? What did you think then?

Well, it's only an opinion, sir.

I'm asking for your opinion. What was it?

I thought he was paying the barman for helping Blank's beer.

And if the word 'pints' was used, it fitted in with that theory, did it not?

Yes, sir.

Then was it not worth mentioning that you thought you'd heard that word?

GEORGE COLMAN, Q.C.

I see it now, sir. But I didn't think so at the time.

What did the man look like?

Oh, he was just an average-looking man. Medium build, dark grey suit. He wore one of those club ties, I think, and a bowler hat.

What club? Or what was the design?

I'm afraid I can't tell you, sir. I'm not even sure that it was a club tie.

Was he a young man or an old one?

It's hard to say. Probably something between the two.

(He's being very vague. I suppose he knows that that description will fit any one of twenty of the defendant's officials. I wonder if he's been hanging about outside the offices.)

Have you seen him since?

No, sir.

Have you made no effort to find out who he was?

I did, but I failed.

Did you perhaps make those efforts by lurking about outside the offices?

You're right, sir. I didn't realize that I'd been noticed.

You claim to be a trained observer. Can you not give me a better description of the man than you have done?

I'm afraid not, sir. I was a bit excited at the time, and I fixed my mind on where he was going, not his appearance.

What were you excited about?

Well, sir, I realized that I now had a valuable piece of evidence. I'd got for my client something better than I'd ever hoped to get.

When did you realize that?

When I saw the money pass.

I have a little difficulty in seeing how that realization can be reconciled with the open mind you were speaking of.

Sir?

CROSS-EXAMINATION

*Never mind. You followed him in a taxi, and saw him enter the offices at
1.47. Is that time correctly stated in your notes?*
Yes, sir. My watch was right early that morning, and still right the
next morning.

**(Now I want him to say that he saw the man go in through the
main door. I'd better try to make him think I want the opposite.)**

Do you think he saw you?
No, sir.
Were you taking any precautions against being noticed?
I made my taxi keep about twenty-five yards behind his.
And when his taxi stopped, were you as far as that behind him?
Yes, sir. We stopped too.
*Then I take it that when you speak of his entering the offices, all you really
mean is that you saw him go through the gate in the iron railings?*
No, sir, I saw more than that.
Are you able to swear that he entered the building?
I am, sir. I saw him do it.
How could you?
As soon as he sent his taxi away and turned his back on the street,
we crept up and I made my taxi stop just beyond the iron gate.
Could you see any of the doors of the building from there?
Yes. The big black door facing the street. He went in through
that door.

(Good. That's what I wanted.)

Did he open the door himself, or did someone let him in?
He ... now let me think. ... I'm not sure, sir.

**(He's getting a bit nervous. I suppose he's wondering why I
asked that question.)**

*Have you, or have you not, a clear picture in your mind of the man
approaching the door and going through it?*

GEORGE COLMAN, Q.C.

(He must say that he has. But I'm afraid he'll be too wary to say that the man just opened the door and walked in.)

I have, sir. But it's hard to say if there was anyone inside the door. I was in no position to see that.

That wasn't what I asked you. Did the man knock, or ring a bell, or just push the door open? You were in a position to see that, weren't you?

Oh! I didn't realize what you wanted. (Slowly)—The man went through the gate in the railings; he took a couple of paces to the steps. ...

Never mind all that. What did he do when he reached the door?

There was a bit of delay at the door, sir, I think. I have a recollection of seeing him fumble with a key. ... I can't be sure. He was between me and the door, more or less.

(He has remembered what time it was. I might as well come out with it now.)

Our evidence will be that everyone in the building left before 1.30 on that Saturday, and that the door you speak of was locked.

I can't dispute that, sir. It fits in with my recollection. He must have let himself in with a key.

Do you see this man? He is the office manager. Is he the man?

No, sir. This gentleman is very old, and rather tall. It was a younger, shorter man.

Look at these two men. They are Mr. Green and Mr. Gray. Was it either of them?

I won't say yes, sir, and I won't say no. I'm not sure, and I'm on oath.

The three men I have had brought into court are the only three people who had keys to the door facing the street on that Saturday afternoon. So I'd like you to tell me, if you possibly can, whether it was one of them?

Then it must have been Mr. Green or Mr. Gray, sir. But I honestly can't say which.

CROSS-EXAMINATION

What will you say if I tell you that Mr. Green was being married, at a church in Scotland, at two o'clock that afternoon. The clergyman, and many other people, if necessary, will swear to that.

That makes it easy, sir. Then it must have been Mr. Gray.

And if I tell you that Mr. Gray was at the wedding?

You're making it difficult for me, sir. ... I can only speak of what I saw. ... How can we be sure that someone didn't have a skeleton key? You must know, sir, that half the thieves in London have them.

Are you suggesting to the court that some thief, unconnected with the defendant firm, bribed a barman to push its beer, and then rushed off to the defendant's offices to write a report about it?

No, sir. It's not for me to speculate, sir, but perhaps one of those three gentlemen lent his key to another member of the firm.

They will say that they did not. Now I must take you back to your visits to the bar.

Counsel now cross-examines on the other incidents in the bar. The witness testifies in accordance with his notes, and nothing new emerges from that part of the cross-examination.

It will be noticed that the cross-examination has not proved anything conclusive about the matters in dispute. One of the three men might have lent his key to another employee, although all three will swear that they did not. The witness could have heard what he claims to have heard in the bar; the denials of the barmen may be false. It has not been shown with certainty that the witness had no connection with the Federal Bureau of Investigation. Still less has it been proved that his claim to have visited the United States was false.

But counsel has achieved a great deal. For one thing, he has put the plaintiff's legal advisers in this difficulty: If they do not call the private detective's wife, their client's case will be open to weighty criticism. But if they do call her, there are many things, arising out of her husband's evidence, which will be put to her; and it is improbable that she will be able to deal with all these things convincingly. There are likely to be conflicts between her testimony and that of her husband. And in any efforts which she may make to avoid such conflicts she will probably have to say things which do not carry conviction, or which will lead her into difficulties of some sort.

Moreover, the private detective himself has been revealed as a shifty, unimpressive witness; the court will have seen that his moral standards are not high; it will have noticed how, in some parts of his evidence, at any rate, he was being evasive. And it will be very sceptical about the honesty of many of his answers, even if they cannot be proved to have been untrue.

Thus, unless the defendant's witnesses are even less satisfactory, the evidence of the private detective is likely to be rejected. The cross-examination was, therefore, a successful one.

Printed in Great Britain
by Amazon